Toronto Reprint Library of Canadian Prose and Poetry

Douglas Lochhead, General Editor

This series is intended to provide for libraries a varied selection of titles of Canadian prose and poetry which have been long out-of-print. Each work is a reprint of a reliable edition, is in a contemporary library binding, and is appropriate for public circulation. The Toronto Reprint Library makes available lesser known works of popular writers and, in some cases, the only works of little known poets and prose writers. All form part of Canada's literary history; all help to provide a better knowledge of our cultural and social past.

The Toronto Reprint Library is produced in short-run editions made possible by special techniques, some of which have been developed for the series by the University of Toronto Press.

This series should not be confused with Literature of Canada: Poetry and Prose in Reprint, also under the general editorship of Douglas Lochhead.

UNIVERSITY OF TORONTO PRESS

Toronto Reprint Library of Canadian Prose and Poetry
© University of Toronto Press 1973
Toronto and Buffalo
Reprinted in paperback 2017
ISBN 978-0-8020-7511-6 (cloth)
ISBN 978-1-4875-9154-0 (paper)

Another edition appeared in 1865
with the joint imprint of:
Montreal, Richard Worthington;
Toronto, Rollo and Adam 1865.
Title page only varies.

THE

ADVOCATE

A NOVEL

BY

CHARLES HEAVYSEGE,

Author of "Saul," "Jephthah's Daughter."

&c., &c., &c.

———— · ⁕ · ————

MONTREAL:

RICHARD WORTHINGTON,

GREAT ST. JAMES STREET.

1865.

M. LONGMOORE & CO., PRINTERS.

THE ADVOCATE.

CHAPTER I.

"Take, oh take those lips away,
That so sweetly were forsworn;
And those eyes, the break of day,
Lights that do mislead the morn:
But my kisses bring again,
bring again
Seals of love, but sealed in vain,
seal'd in vain."

Measure for Measure.

On a bright day during the month of September, of the year 1800, two persons were in earnest conversation in a lawyer's office in the city of Montreal. One of them was the most distinguished advocate of that place; a man of some three score years, and of a commanding yet wild and singular aspect. His companion was a well-dressed female of middle age, and comely, though mournful countenance. Some disagreeable topic seemed to have just ruffled both of their tempers, for her face was moist with tears, and darkened with an expression of disappointment. His own was slightly marked with annoyance, and, suddenly ceasing to arrange some folded law papers that he held in his hands, and had gathered up from the table at which he was standing, he exclaimed in tones of mingled surprise and asperity: " Still at the old song! still harping, harping, harping! Peace, no more of it. Heaven would be insufferable with but

one hymn, hell thrice horrible with but one howl,
earth uninhabitable with but one evil. Oh, variety,
what a charm hast thou!"

"Is this, then, all your answer?" enquired the
female, sorrowfully.

"Is it not decisive?" he demanded sharply.
"Woman, away: am I not busy? Is not this the
very Passion week of preparation before the Easter
of the Assizes?" Then with an upward leer of his
eyes, that were now filled with frolicksome humour,
whilst at the corners of his mouth flickered a grim
smile, he continued: "Mona Macdonald, I am neither
selfish nor sensual, though women call me so; not
prone to be provoked to marriage; though Satan in
your shape has for so many years tempted me thereto,
I have still remained in the bachelors' Eden, in spite
of you and the Serpent. Marry you! Do I look in
the humour for mischief? Do I appear vile enough
to commit the unpardonable sin? No, a man may
put himself beyond the reach of mercy by other means
than that."

Mona looked up and sighed, and he continued:

"What more is marriage than mere desert sands,
in which life's current is lost until it reappears in a
parcel of bubbles called babies. What is it but the
fool's end, the knave's means; a warning to the wise,
a snare to the simple; the wantonness of youth, the
weakness of years; a pillory wherein to exercise
patience; what is it but the Church's stocks for the
wayward feet of women. Marry you! To marry is
to commit two souls to the prison of one body; to put
two pigs into one poke; two legs into one boot, two
arms into one sleeve, two heads into one hat, two

"Do I seem old enough to be a bridegroom?"

necks into one noose, two corpses into one coffin, and
this into a wet grave, for marriage is a perennial
spring of tears. Marry! Why should I bind myself
with a vow that I must break, not being by nature
continent and loving? Marry you! Yes, when I
hate you. Have I a sinistrous look to meditate such
mischief? Do I seem old enough to be a bridegroom?
Pish! I am ashamed to be so importuned."

This badinage was uttered with the fire of youth,
combined with the authority of age, accustomed to
be obeyed, and the listener offered no rejoinder; but
the speaker, having approached, gazed into her eyes
with a twinkling smile of mirth, that gradually
changed to one of fondness and pity ; and kissing her
respectfully, he added in a soft tone : " Come, come,
how is the maid Amanda, how fares our charming
foundling ?"

" Well," was quietly replied.

" Mona, I love that girl," he continued, assuming
a tone of deep sincerity, " for along with the whole
web of your goodness, nature has interwoven into
the fine fabric of her form a thread of my evil—not
in the grosser sense,—no, no; still, look after her;
the breath of passion must be stirring in her, and at
her years most maids are tinder to love's dropping
sparks. Remember, there never yet was a nun but
once had tender thoughts. Love comes unto all that
live, and with not less certainty than death's advances
—nay, even the cold, bony frame of death itself, at
last comes wooing, and elopes with life. Now, home
and cheer your charge." And he playfully pushed
her from the room, then, throwing himself into his
chair, resumed the interrupted study of his briefs.

CHAPTER II.

" A seducer flourishes, and a poor maid is undone.
All's Well That Ends Well.

The advocate was by birth an Englishman, and a cadet of an ancient family, who, after having spent a dissolute youth and early manhood, had come to Canada. Here he became acquainted with an old, half-pay Highland officer of Wolfe's Army, who for his signal services rendered during the operations of the British force before Quebec, had been rewarded with a grant of land in that vicinity. Like others of his countrymen, the Highlander had settled in the Province, and married into a French Canadian family. But, soon after their union, his wife died in giving birth to a daughter, which he reared to womanhood with all the strength of an undivided affection. The Englishman's frank bearing and singular mental powers won the admiration of the old soldier, and, at the same time, dazzled and captivated his comely and unsophisticated daughter, to whom the stranger was soon understood to stand in the light of a lover. But Macdonald—for such was the name of the warm-hearted clansman—was not destined to see his dearest wishes realized in the union of the two. A sudden sickness laid low his hardy frame, and, dying, he called the pair to his bedside, and joined their hands in anticipation of the rite of wedlock. The father dead, the lover betook himself to the study of the

law, and with an extraordinary aptitude and dili-
gence, not only mastered the details of legal practice,
but comprehended, beyond others, the great principles
both of English and of French jurisprudence as prac-
tised in Lower Canada. Ambitious of excellence, he
resolved to complete his studies of the latter in France
itself. Of means he had little, but she, confiding in
his honor, consented that the estate left to her by her
father should be sold, to furnish him with the neces-
sary funds for his maintenance in Paris. In that gay
capital—whilst taking advantage of libraries, and
sitting at the feet of the Gamaliels of the French Bar,
—he associated with gamesters and courtezans, and
was at length left with resources barely sufficient to
enable him to return to Canada. Settling in Montreal,
his extraordinary acquaintance with both schools of
law, his impassioned and versatile eloquence, his ready
repartee, his habitual, grim and grotesque humour,
his outrageous sallies of wit, his unmerciful logic, his
fierce invective, his irony, his sarcasm, and his deep,
irresistible scorn, all heightened by his singularly
expressive personal presence, and eyes kindling with
lambent fire, made him a forensic antagonist with
whom few willingly chose to deal. He soon became
the favorite counsel for the defence. Extensive practice, and its concomitant, a large income, were now
his, and his betrothed, who, in giving him her
fortune, felt as though she had given him nothing
till with it she had given him herself, day by day
looked for the nuptial tie, and at length besought him
to relieve her from what had become a doubtful and
even a dishonorable position. But such was no longer
in his thoughts. Instead of performing towards her

his long plighted vows, he sent her to a lonely dwelling on the then unpeopled Ottawa to hide her shame. There she remained till the scandal of their connection was forgotten, and he brought her, along with her female child, a creature of surpassing beauty, to a new retreat, called Stillyside, bought by him for that purpose, and situated behind the bluff known as Mount Royal, or popularly the "mountain," that lifts its wooded sides in the rear of, and gives name to, the City of Montreal. During these years of their separation, whilst laborious in his profession, he continued to indulge his vein for pleasure; not openly and abroad, as in his earlier days, but in the semisecrecy of his home; and with a still increasing income, his expenditure from this ungracious cause also augmented. Moreover, in those days, the province was, in great measure, ruled by irresponsible officials, and often unscrupulous but energetic adventurers like himself;—men of powerful parts and free lives, whom a community of race, religion, language, and interest, united in a sort of Masonic association, whereof his house became one of the centres of reunion. There, aware of his gentle descent, and impressed with his transcendent abilities; charmed with his conversation—as pithy as it was apt to be impure—his wit, his taste, his information, his judgment; sensible, too, of the excellence of his wines, and luxuriance of his table, around which military officer and civil servant, merchant and judge, were accustomed to assemble, rank and office were forgotten, etiquette laid aside, and abandon ruled the hour. Votaries of Venus and of Bacchus were all of them, however disguised; and, secure in that close conclave,

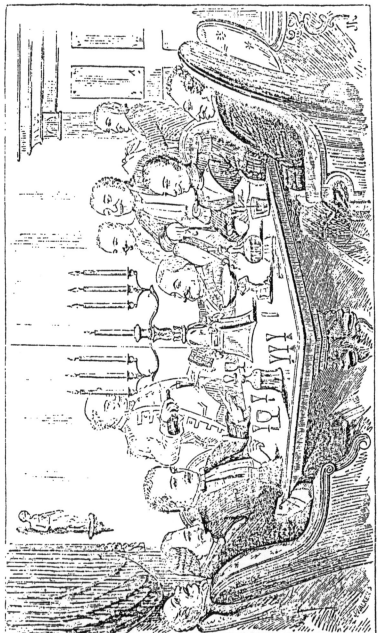

"As if at the jests of another Yorick. raised over the table a long. eruptive roar."

where no pure female presence was found to check the bacchanalian song, or forbid the ribald jest, all sat to listen to and applaud their host's inimitable stories, his grotesque descriptions, his wayward thoughts and fantastic images; to hearken to his close analysis, his robust reasoning, his wondrous pathos, his sublime exaggeration; and, as the wine circulated, to observe yet more his chameleon aspect and Protean character unfold itself; now grovelling like the Paradisal toad, wherein, at the ear of Eve, was hidden the form of Lucifer; now, touched by the Ithuriel spear of some keen conception, suddenly soaring, like to the bright expanded shape of the surprised and fallen Archangel, till the guests themselves, like the startled Ithuriel recoiling from the instant apparition of the fiend, drew back in amazement, or, as if at the jests of another Yorick, raised over the table a long, eruptive roar. Nor was that all. For a moment he would assume the moralist, the theologian, or,—leaving both revelation and the pandects,—become the philosopher, pacing the universe for occult truth; or the metaphysician, tracking the region of the supersensuous; and, over every theme, flying on mocking mental pinions, seeming an intellectual satan, passing through the region of vain questionings and doubtful disquisition, dim out to the abyss. And thus he lived, using, and abusing, his rare gifts; no virtuous and accomplished wife presiding at these feasts, ever degenerating into orgies, or giving sanctity to these walls; within which were gathered the brightest, gayest, noblest, most powerful—often most dissolute—of the land. But now the guests were thinned in numbers by death, by

marriage, by worn out passions; and many a fierce
spirit had been tamed by adversity, till the mirth
had grown to be half moody, and the saturnalia
gross rather in intention than in fact.

Yet ever amidst these distracting pleasures his
heart reverted, first, to the woody wilds of Ottawa,
and afterwards, to the sylvan shades of Stillyside,
which latter he still took delight to visit and adorn;
cherishing its mistress, and watching over and nur-
turing her child, the fruit of her fondness and of his
falsehood;—but commonly known and publicly acknowledged, only as her foster daughter, and, in his
own prouder circle, as his ward. For himself, he
never occupied other than a handsome suburban re-
sidence, situated between the city and the foot of
Mount Royal, and whose doors Mona Macdonald sel-
dom entered; and when she did so, it was to be
scowled upon by its menial mistress, a French Canadian, named Babet Blais, who viewed the melancholy
visitor with angry and jealous eyes. Into this house
many comely Abigails had come and gone; but
Babet Blais remained in spite of him, having, as she
deemed, acquired a wife's settlement and privileges,
by virtue of the presence of a dwarfish, swarthy
creature, half oaf, half imp, their mutual offspring.
This strange being, as if in mockery, for he was ugly
from the womb, was named Narcisse, and flitted
about the house rather than made it his home; rarely
entering it, except in his father's absence, and then
chiefly to obtain largess from his mother, who loved
and indulged him the more because others disliked
or despised him. Reckless, stupid, savage; ignoble
and stubborn; with thick, black, stubby hair, and

dark, bushy, beetling brows; his protuberant eyes filled with cunning, and burning with a lustre like live coals; deep-chested, and with shoulders raised and rounded, giving him an air of pugnacity; snarl written upon his countenance, and pride in the pose of his pygmean figure; dull, dissolute, and disobedient, he was, nevertheless, the idol of his mother. She, poor woman, reverenced, almost worshipped, him, as being something superior to her plebeian self, by reason of the father's part that was in him; wondering how his sire should be so blind to his merits, and so severe upon his alleged faults and foibles. She the rather encouraged him in his irregularities since others rebuked them, and was the more liberal towards him, because of his father's stint; deeming his vices and extravagance to be not only excusable, but proper, in one who had to uphold and play the part of a gentleman. His father strove to instil into him some knowledge of law, but soon relinquished the distasteful and hopeless task, and articled him to a Notary, who, for a tempting premium, consented to take him into his office. But, instead of applying himself there, he spent most of his time in idleness and debauchery; by night frequenting the abodes of vice and infamy, and by day, haunting the doors and corridors of the court-house, in the latter always instinctively seeking to avoid a rencontre with his sullen and offended parent.

CHAPTER III.

"Haply despair hath seized her."
Cymbeline.

It was now evening, and the landscape lay steeped
in yellow sunshine; when Mona Macdonald rode
slowly homewards, silent and buried in gloom. Her
way lay around the base of the mountain. But neither its adjacent and majestic sides on the one hand,
nor the placid, mellow-tinted, and sky-bounded plain
on the other were regarded by her. Her thoughts
were still with the advocate in his office, or with
her departed father in her native home below Quebec, as he and she had lived and loved each other
there, nearly twenty years before. Thus preoccupied, she lent no heed to the landscape, although before her was the broad, descending sun, and behind
her was the mighty Saint Lawrence basking in bur-
nished gold; and soon another stream, a branch of the
Ottawa, appeared in the distance, the two clasping between them as in a zone the Island of Montreal.
But neither the note of birds, the lowing of cattle,
the barking of dogs, the churr of the bullfrog, the
distant human voices coming faintly over the lea, nor
yet the elysean landscape were seen or heard; and
not until the carriage drew up at Stillyside, and the
bark of a lap-dog, on the top of the distant steps,
that led to the verandah in front of the house, struck
her ear, did she fully awake from her mournful reverie. Then, alighting, she passed through a postern

that hung at the side of folding gates, and, winding
her way up a walk bordered with shrubs and flowers,
approached the dwelling, that stood upon a knoll.
At that moment the sound of a cowbell in the contiguous mountain coppice told the slow approach of a
dappled dairy, in charge of a swarthy French Canadian youth. All else was quiet about the place, that
seemed to be lying in a sort of listless, half dreamy
tranquillity and halcyon repose. The mansion itself
was spacious, and built of the grey limestone of the
district. Woodbine and hop, clematis and the Vir-
ginia creeper half concealed its rugged exterior, and
clothed in tangled luxuriance the verandah that
extended along the front. The roof was covered
with shingles, painted red; and in it were a number
of dormer windows, which, like all the other windows, were hidden with closed green blinds or shutters. Swallows were darting about the eaves, and
wheeling around a fountain and jet d'eau in front,
that were fed by a mountain spring behind the
house; whilst from one of the rather numerous chim-
neys a frail wreath of blue smoke crept, and
lingered lazily about the lightning rod, before it
rose and melted away into the pure evening sky.
But by this time the lap-dog had come forwards to
meet her, and now ran in advance, emitting a fitful
and joyous bark; and as she ascended the steps the
door was opened by a servant, who, having admitted
her, closed it again; but not before a stranger might,
from without, have witnessed a fair and youthful female figure swiftly descend the stairs into the hall,
and, throwing her arms around the neck of the returned traveller, greet her with an affectionate sa-

lute.   A large, grey mastiff now appeared from the
rear of the building, and, while the driver was
removing sundry parcels from the carriage, took a
few slow and solemn turns about the knoll, then, on
the departure of man and vehicle, retired for the
night to his kennel, leaving the scene as quiet as before.

CHAPTER IV.

"Ungracious wretch,
Fit for the mountains, and the barbarous caves
Where manners ne'er were preached! Out of my sight."
Twelfth Night.

On the morning of the following day, Mona Macdonald sat at breakfast in a room at Stillyside. She was plainly and neatly dressed; and with her sat a figure more lady-like, and still in her teens, attired simply, but with negligent taste. Both seemed abstracted, and, as they silently sipped their tea, appeared to be brooding over some recent, sad subject of conversation. The weather, too, without, was as sombre as the mood within. A canopy of cold, grey clouds covered the sky; the air was chilly, and the wind swayed the trees to and fro, betokening rain. From time to time the cat, with arched back, and tail erect, came loudly purring, and rubbing its sleek sides against the skirts of its mistresses; the lap-dog was restless; and upon the hearthrug a drowsy spaniel lay with his nose between his paws, and whined fitfully in a dog's day-dream; whilst the females, at length altogether ceasing to eat, sat self-absorbed. On the face of the elder was an expression of sorrow tempered with patience, but on that of the younger, an air of melancholy was mingled with resentment, that heightened almost into majesty a form and countenance of extraordinary and statuesque beauty. From time to time her companion regarded her with a look of anxiety and tenderness, and at length, seeing her still abstaining from the suspended meal, exclaimed:

"Eat, child, eat: fasting is bad for the young."

"I have no appetite, except for information," was mournfully replied; and the elder again regarded her affectionately; then with subdued earnestness, and in an expostulatory tone, rejoined:

"Be pacified, Amanda; for curiosity often brings us care. Let well alone, and it will continue to be well with you; but why should you thus persist to peer into the bottom of your past; as it were, asking the fashion of your swaddling clothes? Fie! you are too impatient; too importunate. Pray, no longer question me against my will, making enquiries that may not be answered. Live without asking why you live. No more of this. Does not your guardian love you as though you were his child; and is he not wiser than yourself; to judge of what knowledge is for your welfare? You ask me, why this mystery about your birth. Amanda, we move midst mystery from birth to death, and they who seek to solve it seek for sorrow."

"These words disturb me more than your past silence," exclaimed the younger. "What horror is there to reveal touching my origin, that you yet dare not shew me?"

"I dare not break your guardian's command," replied the elder, firmly.

"Neither can I control a natural desire to know what so nearly concerns me," retorted the other. "I beg of you to solve this mystery of my birth. It is my right, my birthright, to know who gave me birth. It is said that I was found—where was I found? by whom? how have I been confided to your care? by whose appointment have I had given to me this guardian? and why is he so kind, and wherefore are you so faithful? Tell me, nurse, why has he caused me to be educated with such care; from what motive has he caused me to be furnished with accomplishments that seem to reach beyond the bounds of my prospective sphere? Nurse, I charge you,—if you indeed have nursed me from my birth, as you declare you have done,—tell me, I pray you tell me: it is not much to ask: the very poorest child yet knows its parentage; the meanest beggar knows whether his father once asked alms or not; but I know nothing of my progenitors; whether they were of a proud or of a humble station, whether good or vicious; whether they be yet living or be long since dead. I do not know even whether my guardian knew them, nor how he has come to be my guardian, my kind supporter, friend: nothing do I know of these, whose all I ought to know. What is the reason of this singular secrecy? Nurse, tell me all you know,—for well I know you know,—tell me, I say, about my parentage; declare, again I charge you, and now most solemnly, if you really love me, who gave me to your care and to his kind tutelage: Nurse, Mona, foster-mother, speak; how have I become the ward, nay, like the very child, of that eccentric, wise, gay, good old man?"

"More gay than good, and not so wise as wicked," muttered Mona, and, not giving her companion time to reply, continued:

"Amanda, do not importune me further, I conjure

B

you. Enough for you to know your guardian loves
you, cherishes you even as if you were his child.
Let us arise from table since our meal seems done;—
what is it that alarms you? Ah! And at that moment the report of a gun, the crashing of a window
pane, the sound of shot hurtling past, its striking the
opposite wall of the apartment, and dropping, along
with falling plaster, on to the floor, burst upon them;
followed, without, by the expostulating tones of a
man-servant, that were soon overpowered by a loud
guffaw, and, before the interlocuters had recovered
from their astonishment and terror, Narcisse, followed by several men carrying fowling pieces, rushed,
swearing, into the vestibule. Amanda saw him,
and, rising to her feet, regarded him through the
doorway with a look of scorn and anger akin to that
cast by the Belviderean Apollo upon the wounded
Python. But his dull temperament was invulner-
able to the arrows that shot from her eyes, and, un-
daunted, he swept forward into the room, and with
coarse familiarity attempted to salute her. He was
unsuccessful, for Mona, advancing between them,
hindered the nearer approach of the intruding mannikin, who, baffled, and with the eyes of Amanda
still fixed upon him, and yet beaming ineffable contempt and disdain, at length stood before her with
downcast look, like one detected in some act of guilt.
His companions one by one slunk back to the lawn,
whither in the dumb disgrace of his discomfiture, he
followed them. There, meeting with the domestic
already mentioned, and who had now been joined by
a fellow-servant; first an altercation, then a scuffle
ensued, in which latter the mastiff took an effective

part, in maintaining the equality of the house against
what otherwise would have been overwhelming odds;
but he was at last disabled by a blow with the butt
of a fowling-piece, whilst the lap-dog, as it stood barking on the borders of the fray, was shot dead by the
cowardly and vindictive Narcisse. This was too
much to be borne, and, indignant, the ladies descended to the lawn. At the same moment, three female domestics appeared upon the scene, and changed
the character of the encounter. Three brawny ruf-
fians seized each an Abigail, and attempted to bear
her off, as of old the treacherous Roman bachelors
carried the Sabine maids. Screams filled the air,
mingled with oaths and laughter; and the affair that
had been begun in vulgar, aimless, frolic, might
have ended in serious outrage, but just then a horseman appeared at the gate, dismounted, and, rushing
in, riding-whip in hand, plied it with such vigor,
that in a few seconds all the rude gang had fled except Narcisse, who, having stumbled, was seized by
the collar, hurried forward, and spurned through the
gateway into the road, leaving his fowling-piece behind him.

The stranger now for the first time seemed to observe the ladies, and bowing to them respectfully, for
a moment appeared to hesitate whether to approach
and address them. They, too, stood silent, but it
was with mixed astonishment and agitation, and
he still stood regarding the younger with an expression of deep admiration; till, as if suddenly recollecting himself, and bowing yet more profoundly than
before, accompanied with an apologetic smile, en-
hancing the beauty of his young and noble coun-

tenance, he gracefully retired to his steed, vaulted into the saddle, and, galloping away, was soon hidden from their view by a turn in the road.

"Oh, nurse, Mona, we have been rude indeed!" then exclaimed the younger: "We have committed the most odious of all sins, ingratitude; and," she added half archly, "we have seen the noblest of all forms, Mona, a gentleman. Nay, but to have let the chivalrous stranger, our deliverer, depart without a word of grateful recognition;—who will champion us the next time, good Mona."

"May we never again require such timely help, child," replied her mentor: "But let us go within and ascertain the damage that has been done there by these vagabonds from the city;" and, so saying, she took up the dead lap-dog and carried it tenderly in upon her arm, viewing it with a wistful expression of grief and pity, whilst Amanda stooped to caress the wounded mastiff, then followed with an air of pensive majesty, not without looking in the direction in which the gallant stranger had disappeared.

CHAPTER V.

" An ill-favored thing, sir, but mine own."

As You Like It.

It was near mid-day, and the advocate was engaged in his office, when the notary with whom Narcisse had been placed, suddenly entering, angrily demanded :

" Where is Narcisse, where is your son, sir ? Here I am wanting his assistance, now, and he is missing, he is gone, no one knows where, nor where he has stowed those papers. Where is he, sir ; where is the boy, I say ; where is your son ?"

The advocate looked up at this sudden disturbance, and, drawing a deep sigh, exclaimed with bitter emphasis :

" I would he were nowhere ; that he were erased from the book of being ; I would he were in heaven, —or else—in your office, Monsieur Veuillot. Is that a bad wish for either ?"

" But he is not in my office," said Veuillot.

" Nor in heaven neither, I fear," rejoined the advocate.

" Where is he, then ?" demanded the excited notary : " where is your son ?"

" Such a son ! murmured the advocate, shrugging his shoulders. " Do you wish to be pleasant with me, Monsieur Veuillot ? my evil genius call him. Son !

I own I feed him, as I do other vermin that infest my house."

"But where is he?" reiterated the notary with growing impatience, and seeming resolved to take no denial.

"Where is he?" echoed the advocate: "ask his mother; yes, sir, ask his dam. Oh, Monsieur Veuillot, is there not deep damnation in thus having an idiot for one's child? Here is your purgatory — purgatory? no: for purgatory is a kind of half-way house to heaven, but this son of mine is to me a slippery stepping-stone to perdition. Sir, a child should be a cherub to lift its parents' spirit to the skies; but mine, oh!"—and a spasm of agony passed over the old man's visage, succeeded by a forced expression of calmness, as he continued:

"Veuillot, you have heard of Solomon. He speaks of the foolish son of a wise father. He was himself the father of a fool, that rent the kingdom, —Rehoboam I mean,—and he kept concubines, too; so I suppose he waxed fruitful in fools. I have but one fool, therefore I am thankful;—but then he is a thorough fool, a most unmitigated, and unmitigatable fool; the fool of fools, a finished fool, the pink of fools; a most preposterous, backwards-going, crab-like fool; a filthy fool; an idiot, sir, without either parts or particle of ambition; an ape, an owl that flits about by day; a bat, and a bad bat, that flits from tavern to sty; chief of the devil's nightingales; a raven that, roving to foul roosts, goes beating the bosom of the night; a soul that loves the darkness; a mole, sir, a blind mole; a piece of animated perversity, a creature that persists to go astray."

"Where has he strayed to now?" demanded the notary.

"Into the hands of justice, perhaps;" was the fierce reply : " into the grip of the law; up to the foot of the gallows; on to the hill of my extreme disgrace."

" Where is he, where can I find him ? tell me only where," cried Veuillot.

" Where! let echo answer,—would you wish to hunt him ?" said the advocate, mocking. "Did you ever gallop, sir, after a hedgehog ? have you assisted to draw a badger? I am badgered by him, and will blame him, ay, ban him, for he is my curse, my bane; why should I not curse him as Noah cursed that foul whelp Canaan ? Beshrew him for a block-head, a little black-browed beetle, a blot of ink, a shifting shadow, a roving rat, a mouse, yes, sir, a very mouse, that creeps in and out of its hole when the old cat is away. Away, Mr. Notary, away; go, good Monsieur Veuillot. There are more concep-tions in man than he has yet expressed either in sta-tutes or in testaments. Go; you are a deed-drawer; I'll be a deed doer : I'll do, I'll do,—I do not know what I'll do, but something shall be done. He shall be shaken over perdition; sent to grind in the prison house; sold into slavery :—fool! he shall be banished to Caughnawaga, or to Loretto ;—the further the bet-ter; he shall be sent to the Lake of the Two Moun-tains, sir, or to Saint Regis to learn the war-whoop and gallant the squaws. You smile :—but to your er-rand, Veuillot; it is not known where my son is: I saw him last night, may I never see him again! Then, dying, my old age, perhaps, may close in peace : not else, not else."

The notary departed, but the exasperated lawyer
still conversed with himself. "I cannot decently
die," he said, "any more than I can devoutly live,
pricked through the very reins and kidneys with
that skewer. Alas! he is my goad, my thorn in the
flesh, the messenger of satan sent to buffet me. He
is the mosquitto that stings my knuckles; the little,
black, abominable fly that will insist to assail my
nose; he is my bruise, my blain, my blister, my
settled, ceaseless source of irritation : the cause,
the cause—of what is he the cause? Alas! that
I should ever have been the cause of such a foul
effect! But let it be so; the whitest skins have
moles, the sun has spots; he is my mole, my spot;
and I, I am the father of the fool, Narcisse."

Narcisse was that moment at a tavern in the beautiful village of Cote des Neiges, adjacent to Stillyside, and much resorted to by pleasure seekers from
Montreal. His companions, too, were there, bewail-
ing the loss of one of their fowling-pieces, and devis-
ing means for revenge on their interrupter and successful assailant. There they remained, and, instead
of spending the day, as was their first intention, on
the side of the mountain, in popping at small birds,
they passed many of its hours in quaffing large potations, the effects of which they in some degree slept
off by a long afternoon nap. It was now nightfall,
and they were returning homewards, conversing
in loud and angry tones on the humiliation of the
morning, and threatening retribution against its
cause, the gallant stranger. Narcisse, with the liti-
giousness of his maternal race, and prompted by his
inkling of law, was for launching an action for assault

and battery against their assailant's purse, whilst the others, pot-valiant, declared their anxiety to meet him in bodily conflict on another field; and thus discoursing in the deepening gloom, the party arrived opposite the mansion at Stillyside. For a few moments they halted, undetermined whether to approach, and demand the delivery of the captured weapon; but at last agreed to waive the requisition, chiefly at the instance of Narcisse, who authoritatively ruled, that to demand and accept of the feloniously acquired gun, would be to compound a felony. Hereupon, being somewhat more at ease in their minds, they proceeded, and now less noisily, continuing on their way with only occasional bursts of abuse, and the firing off of fag ends of French songs, accompanied with a fitful fusilade of low, horselaughter; and thus, mollified and maudlin, unsteadily continued their straggling march, until they halted at a gate on the roadside, and some distance behind which, loomed a large, dingy and deserted-looking dwelling, half concealed by tall trees. No light was to be seen, but, after a brief consultation, the party swung open the gate, entered, and having reached the house, one of the number gave a peculiar tapping at a window, followed by a low whistle or call, that was immediately answered by a corresponding sound from within, and this again by a counter signal, which was repeated like the faintly returning tone of an echo; and, after some delay, the door slowly opened, the voices of men and women, mingling in boisterous mirth, burst forth like the roar of a suddenly opened furnace, the party entered, and the door was closed again.

CHAPTER VI.

" How now, you secret, black, and midnight hags ?"

Macbeth.

At the same hour that Narcisse and his companions entered the sombre and suspicious looking dwelling, the advocate returned to his home in the upper environs of the city, wearied in mind and frame, from an application broken only by the entrance of Monsieur Veuillot, and the arrival of a messenger from Stillyside, who, hot and excited from the violent scene whereof it had been the theatre, painted the outrage in deepened colors, and exaggerated form. Anger and shame contended in the old lawyer's bosom as he heard the story; the former sentiment urging for the punishment of the delinquents, the latter pleading for forbearance; for amongst the transgressors was his illegitimate son, whose share in the offence, if brought into the light of the tribunal, would thence cast back a shadow upon the father, and point, publicly and anew, to their disreputable relationship. Others also, whose reputation was far dearer to him than his own, must be dragged, either as witnesses or as prosecutrix, to public gaze, and thus be made to furnish matter for the tongue of scandal. Perhaps, too, some latent paternal tenderness inclined the incensed advocate to mercy; and, giving the messenger a hastily written note, sympathizing with the tenants of Stillyside, he despatched

him thither, along with a noble Newfoundland
dog, then lying in the office, and which he meant
should replace the disabled mastiff. Afterwards, his
thoughts, occupied with the important professional
business of the day, scarcely reverted to the vexa-
tious occurrence of the morning; but now, at eve, the
tide of attention, that had been so long dammed
back, came flowing over his spirit with increasing
depth and force; and, in spite of his unwillingness
and the necessity for recruiting his wasted energies,
for the performance of the onerous public duties of
the morrow, he fell to brooding over the new mis-
deed of the already too obnoxious Narcisse. From
the son, his musings reverted to the menial mother,
and, by contrast, from her to the fair tenants at
Stillyside; till, tossed by the contrary and vexed
tides of thought and feeling, he arose, perturbed from
the lounge, went to the window, and, drawing aside
the curtains, beheld in the east the full moon climbing the clear, blue heavens, amidst a multitude of
marble clouds. Struck with sudden admiration and
oblivious pleasure, he opened the folding frames and
stepped into the garden. The air was balmy; and,
soothed by the change, he returned within, reas-
sumed the habiliments of the day, took a stout,
ivory-headed walking cane from its corner, and,
calling a domestic, announced that he should for
some time be absent. His first impulse was to cross
a contiguous, half-reclaimed tract, sprinkled with
vast boulders of the glacial period, and reach the
turnpike road that led around the mountain. But
before he turned to commence his stroll he paused to
gaze down on the outstretched city, that, lying as

asleep on the arm of the St. Lawrence, with tin-covered domes, spires, cupolas, minarets, and radiant roofs, showing like molten silver in the moonbeams, contrasting with the dark shingles covering most of the houses, presented an enchanted-looking scene of glory and of gloom. On the left, and oldest of its class, was the Bonsecours Church, with its high-pitched roof, and airy, but inelegant, campanile, refulgent as if cut from some rock of diamond. Nearer, was the Court House, and, beneath it, the Jail; and, behind them both, the dusky expanse of the poplar-planted Champ de Mars. In the midst of the city rose the tin-mailed tower and spire of the French Cathedral, and, at its rear, loomed the neighboring, wall-girt, solemn Seminary of Saint Sulpice. The bright, precipitous roof of the Church of the Recollets, and the spangled canopy of the vast foundation of the Grey Nuns reposed resplendent; and, within its ample enclosure, luminous as a moon-lit lake, the quadrangled and cloistered College of Montreal. Beyond these, in the midst of the shining river, duskily slumbered the little, fortified and wooded Island of Sainte Helene; and up the stream, apast the petty promontory of Pointe Saint Charles, stretched the low, umbrageous lapse of Nuns Island, whence the eye followed the bending flood, that trended towards where, with eternal toil and sullen roar, agonize for ever the hoary rapids of Lachine. In the other direction the eye roved downwards over Hochelaga and Longueuil, Longue Pointe and Pointe aux Trembles, towards where lay the islet-strewn shallows of Boucherville, and, lower yet, the village of Varennes. The mountains of Boucherville, Belœil,

Chambly, and Vermont shadowy bounded the horizon; and, turning from these, abrupt before him rose
the awful and spectral presence of Mount Royal.
Skirting its foot he now proceeded, brushing away the
shining dew, disturbing the lazy lizard and the sere-
nading grasshopper, and hearing below him the harsh
croaking of the bullfrog in the pool; whilst, ever and
anon, the gust awoke, with a huge sigh, the dreaming maples, poplars, and dark, penitential pines.
From the remote, secluded farms came the faint bark
of dogs; and amidst such sights and sounds he at
length emerged upon the winding road, that, if followed, would lead him past Stillyside. Slowly and
without special aim he continued to walk, ruminating and still drawn onwards, lured by the time and
scene, until the sound alike of mastiff and of cur had
ceased, the grasshopper refused to pipe upon the
dusty road, and the too distant bullfrog was no
longer heard gurgling to its mates, but all was silent,
lying as in a trance, both heaven and earth. And
then he paused, and lapsing into meditation, stood
unconscious of surrounding things, till the tolling of
the clock in the distant tower of the cathedral of
Notre Dame awoke him, and, starting from his reverie and listening, he counted the hours to the full
score of midnight. Struck, then, by the weird aspect of the scene and singular silence, a vague sense
of horror stole through him, and he exclaimed
hoarsely: "This is the very witching time of night,
when churchyards yawn and spirits walk abroad!"
and scarcely had the words escaped his lips when
a wild tumult rose near him, and he perceived a
bacchanalian and disorderly troop of both sexes

sallying into the moonlight; wherein with uncouth
antics and inviting pose, they disported towards
a group of trees, encircling which, and in the
chequered beams beneath their boughs, he beheld
them in Harlequin and Columbine-like appeals of
passion, or already mated and forming for the medi-
tated measure ; appearing the very gang of Circe;—
and in their midst he now observed his son, the
brutish looking, cunning, and sensual Narcisse, wine-
flushed and loud, and seeming to be the mimic Comus
of the crew. As with the power of divination,
he at once comprehended the spectacle. He had arrived opposite the equivocal building wherein Narcisse and his companions had disappeared some hours
before, and the door of which had just been suddenly
flung open, and kindling with wrath he at once
advanced upon the bacchants in the midst of their
orgies. At the same instant, from the direction of
the city and unseen by him, a tall rider on a lofty
steed, cloak flying to the breeze, swept by like an
apparition; greeted only with a comical yell of
astonishment and derision from one of the females,
as like a spectre it swept by. But the hilarious band
before him was too much preoccupied with the performance of its mockeries to have observed anything,
and the advocate, with eyes gleaming and fixed upon
his son, who now perceiving him stood terror stricken,
approached the revellers, who subsided before him, as,
with grey hair fluttering in the wind, he came
beneath the extending boughs, like some denouncing
Druid amidst the sacred oaks, his countenance in-
flamed, his whole frame seeming to shake as if in
throes to eject some foul possession ; or, rather, as if

he were himself a fierce, incarnate, and unfriendly spirit; and, at length, addressing his son, who was now leaning against a tree, both for support and concealment, he burst forth : "Miscreant !"—and the word was echoed from the side of a huge, dilapidated barn,—"Wretches," he hollowed; and the guilty crowd, fearing both individual recognition and personal contact, again began to retire.

"Stay," he commanded, imperiously, "you are known, and flight shall put the worst construction on your case;—halt, brawlers and bullies, spendthrifts and bankrupts, breakers of the peace; sons of afflicted parents, husbands of weeping wives, brothers of sisters both ashamed and grieved; outlaws; the city's scum, the country's scourge, the harvest that shall yet be reaped for the jail, and leave gleanings for the gallows; abandoned creatures, linger; " and suddenly grasping Narcisse: "Sirrah," he cried, "here is your nightly haunt, these are your companions,—come with me, sir, come,—ah, will you resist your"—father he was about to say, but he recoiled from the word as from an adder, and, casting upon his son a look of unspeakable disdain, he shook the writhing criminal, who the next moment escaped from his hold, and slunk away, still looking backward over his shoulder and muttering curses upon his begetter. The advocate stood watching him in silence, as, withdrawing along with the others, the distance dimmed his form, and drowned his maledictions; then, drawing a deep sigh, a dark, vindictive scowl gathered upon his visage, until its expression became diabolical, and these words rolled from his heaving chest in deep, irregular murmurs:

" Thou son of a wicked and rebellious woman, do
I not know that thou hast set my friends against me,
and caused mine enemies to hold me in derision!
But thou shalt suffer, thou shalt bend, or I will
break thee, yea, dash thee into pieces. May not the
potter do what he wills with the cup his own hands
have fashioned? Away with thee, misshapen reptile; may soon the Saint Lawrence hide thee, or
may'st thou soon be laid in the burial field of thy
mother's race. Away, thou vessel of dishonor; grant
Heaven that I may not yet make of thee a vessel of
wrath!" and the old man's countenance worked convulsively, as he seemed to be revolving some terrible idea; but at last growing calmer he exclaimed:
" Down, down, ye cruel thoughts, ye horrible con-
ceptions; hence, busiest suggestions of the fiend;
be silent at my ears, ye visionary lips; ye perilous
and importunate prompters, peace!" But scarcely
had he uttered these words, when a report of firearms sounded amongst the trees, and a shot rattled
through the boughs, scattering the leaves upon his
head; and the replicated echoes had hardly ceased,
when a peal of triumphant laughter rose, and continued to be renewed till the spot appeared a field for
the sport of a hundred goblins of mischief.

" Come in," at length said a voice, and, turning, he
beheld a woman standing in the doorway.

" Who are you?" he enquired.

" Enter, and learn;" she answered: "I would not
have you murdered in your old age. Do you not
know me?" and seizing him rudely she drew him
towards her until his face almost touched her own
emaciated countenance, on which played a sardonic

smile as she turned it towards the moonlight, and he strove to free himself, exclaiming:

"Witch, hag, loose me:" and gazed upon her with a look of mingled amazement and abhorrence.

"Am I then so changed?" she demanded, with a gloomy smile; "am I become a leper; am I grown loathsome now, whom you once declared to be so lovely? Follow me, false man; you did not once require solicitation." And again the sound of firearms startled the night, and once more the leaves fell fluttering on his head, and the beldam angrily exclaimed: " Come in, old fool," and laid hands on him a second time, as, in a voice thick and hurried with dislike and terror, he replied: " You are remembered by me, woman; give me shelter for a moment," and hastily stepping with her over the threshhold, she closed the door after them. Another burst of triumphant laughter rose from the retiring revellers, and again moonlight and returning silence rested on the scene.

c

CHAPTER VII.

"It is my lady: oh, it is my love!"
Romeo and Juliet.

The agitation of the morning at Stillyside had subsided as the day wore, but the mind of Amanda Macdonald (for such was the name of the younger and fairer denizen of that sequestered abode) remained pensive and preoccupied; and when at her usual hour she had ascended to her chamber, instead of retiring to rest, she took up a tale of the troubadours, and read; nor did she lay down the volume till the sudden flickering of the candle in the socket and the simultaneous tolling from the distant belfry of the church of the village of Saint Laurent warned her that it was midnight. Then, feeling oppressed, alike with the heaviness of the atmosphere of her room, and a strange weight at her heart, analogous to the lassitude that is sometimes felt in the beginning of sickness, she arose, drew aside the curtains, and throwing open the folding window, stepped on to the verandah. A clear Canadian night, appearing a new and chaster version of the day, greeted her. The moon, at night's meridian, hung high in the fulness of its autumnal splendor, tranquil in the solitude of the sky, a solitude unbroken, save by a few small stars that were twinkling in the azure, and a fleet of low, dappled clouds that were coasting the horizon. Awhile her eyes dwelt abstractedly on the sight, then, falling, they wandered listlessly over the broad and shining expanse of landscape before her; where Nature, unrobed, seemed as in a bath; for in front, the grass, steeped in descending dews, glittered as a lake. Woods confined the view in one direction, and the gleamy wave of the Ottawa, amidst filmy obscurity, bounded it, yet further off, in another. Unseen but felt, like the unperceived Genius of the landscape, towered close behind her the sombre-sided mountain; and, touched by the solemn scene, she advanced, and, leaning upon the balustrade, heaved a deep sigh; then lapsed into a reverie so profound, that she failed to hear the tramp of a horse now rapidly approaching, and to note the change to sudden silence, caused by its stopping at the postern. But there, transfixed with wonder and admiration, and looking like a bronze equestrian statue at the gate, now, mounted, sat gazing the lately flying horseman of the road, the champion of the morning on those grounds, and contemplated the figure on the verandah; then, dismounting, tied his steed, and vaulting over the fence, swiftly approached across the lawn; till, as if suddenly aware of being on holy ground, he paused, and stood with reverential aspect and clasped hands, eagerly bending towards her as if in adoration. Thus engaged, as stands in ecstasy some newly arrived pilgrim before a shrine, he stood enrapt; whilst she remained as moveless as a carved angel leaning over a cathedral aisle, and, with her eyes fixed on vacancy, at length mournfully exclaimed:

"Sad, sad, so sad!—yet why am I so sad? No denser grows the mystery around my birth; and if

knight errants yet live, rescuing maids, or he is a
wandering god, and here is Arcadia, why should
that make me grieve? It is true that he is handsome—and yet what of that?—most men are handsome in the eyes of maids. But he appears the paragon of men. Is he indeed not all a man should
be? Where were the blemish, the exception; who
shall challenge nature, saying, in his form, that here
she has given too little, there too much?—Ah, me!
I am not happy, yet I should be so."

"Can I have heard aright, or do I dream?" gasped
out the stranger.

"A knight, a god;" she continued, yet musing;
"oh, he came hither like a knight of old, or as
an angry angel sent to scatter fiends;—or, rather,
like the lightning he arrived, out of the storm-cloud
of I know not where. Where is he now? whence
was he? who is he? what? Alas, I know nothing
of where, nor who, nor what, nor whence he is;
all that I know is, I am strangely sad; and that such
perfection was not made for me."

"Is this not Stillyside?" enquired the listener, "or
do I wander in some spirit-land; lost, lost;—oh,
so luxuriously lost! She, too, seems lost— lost in
a reverie, and all forlorn. I'll speak to her;—and
yet I fear to speak, I fear to breathe, lest the undu-
lating air should burst this, and prove it to be but a
bubble. Yet she breathes, she spoke, and oh, such
words! Words, be at my command; I will address
her, for this is not fancy: could fancy shew a moving
soul of sorrow? See how the passion plays upon
that face, as she thus stands with sad-eyed earnestness, maintaining converse with the hollow sky.

Looked ever aught so fair yet so forlorn ? Methinks
there is a tear upon her cheek. Why comes it from
the Eden of her eye ? I must speak to her ;" and with
mixed fear and fervour he exclaimed : " May Heaven
keep you from grave cause of sorrow, lady ! Forgive
me, oh, forgive me, lady, or vision, for, by these
dazzled eyes, and, as I fear, by your offended form,
I scarcely can divine whether you are of earth or
air ; pardon me if I have appeared here by night, as
unpremeditatedly as I came by day. Bid me begone,
—and yet permit me to remain, for, by my life, and
the deep admiration with which you have inspired
me, I cannot leave you till I learn your grief, and
with it, peradventure, my own doom. Whom did
you speak of even now, fair form ?"

" Who asks of me that question ; who is it that
thus listens when I thought myself alone ?" she
demanded haughtily, looking downwards from the
verandah. " Sir, just now I spoke, and said—I
know not what. What you have overheard me say
I fear was foolish ; do not, then, regard it. I know
you now. You are the stranger who, this morning,
drove those violent intruders from these grounds.
Ah, who would have thought you would return
by night, and thus, sir, play the eaves-dropper ! Oh,
for shame ! Nay, you are not the one I took you for.
Sir, it is mean to overlisten ; mean, very mean ; nay,
it is base, unmanly, to listen to a maid, when she
commits her vagaries to the moon."

" Scourge me, for I deserve it, with your tongue ;"
rejoined the stranger—" but, lady, you were not alone,
though I were absent ; no ; you cannot be alone.
Such excellence must draw hither elves and mid-

night troops of fairies; by day, by night, each moment must array around you the good wishes of the
world. No, not alone; the very sky is filled with
watchers and the ground covered with invisible
feet, that have come here to do you homage; then
why not I found here to pay you mine? Are you
still angry?"

"You have offended me," she answered;—" and
yet perhaps I am too severe with you. I fear I am
ungrateful. 'Mean,' did I say? It was mean in me
to say so, and most forgetful of the favor conferred
here by you this morning. No, I vow it was not
mean—at least in *you*. And yet it was mean, it
was very mean in you, sir, thus to overstep the golden mean of manners. Scourge you? Ah, I fear you
well deserve it;—and yet if I could, I would put to
scourging that word, 'mean,' that has just escaped
from out of my petulent lips, as sometimes a froward,
disobedient child runs into danger, breaking away
from out of the nurse's arms. But you should not
have played the bold intruder, and joined in these
vain vigils;—nay, begone, or I must, myself, withdraw. I do entreat you, stay no longer; come some
other time,—but go to-night; make no excuse for
staying, or you may yet compel me to be angry with
you. Indeed, I fear that I am too forgiving. Go, I
pardon you,—but go at once, or I may yet repent
to have condoned what it, in truth, were hard to
justify."

"Heaven pardons heavier sins," observed the
stranger.

"Yes, when its pardon is sought for;" was rejoined; "but I pardon you without your craving

it; and, remember, Heaven's pardon is not granted
to us simply for the asking; neither do we receive it
because our hearts are penitent; but for the sake
of Him who died for us upon the cross; hence you
are now forgiven by me, not for your prayers' sake,
nor for your regret, but rather because beforehand,
the night's offence has been cancelled by the morning's favor. For the rest, retire, sir: what you
have heard, you have heard. You have heard my
words, yet give no heed to them. If I to-night
have walked forth in my sleep, and dreamed on this
verandah;—why, then, it was but a dream. Let it
be thus esteemed, and so we part. Good night."

"Stay!" exclaimed the stranger, as, smiling with
ineffable sweetness, and deeply curtsying, she
drew backwards towards the window : "Stay; how
can those part whom destiny hath joined; how
be divided whom their fates make one ? Stay, lady,
and let love, young love, plead his own cause. Oh,
I would yet charm you with my tongue, even as
your own detected tongue has just declared that
this morning I charmed you with my deed. Stay.
If, in truth, you did admire, what, at the moment of
its execution, I thought nothing of, and value now
only as it has relation to yourself, hear my appeal."

"What does this mean ?" she asked, startled at
his earnestness : "I do not know you ; go, oh, go ; I
say again, I do not know you, sir."

"I never knew myself till now," he cried with
bitter pathos.

"I say, I do not know you ; you do not know
me;" she reiterated.

"Know me to be irrevocably yours ;" rejoined the

stranger, "for you have bound my heart in such fast thraldom, that even yourself could not deliver it."

"And, perhaps, I would not, if I could,—unless you asked it :" she answered : "and yet, sir, possibly you jest. Oh, sir, forbear ; begone, nor longer fool here a surprised, lone girl. What is your purpose ? who, and whence, are you ? On your honor, answer me truly."

"I am the seigneur Montigny's only son : my purpose and my thoughts towards you are all honorable :" he replied. And she rejoined : "Oh, if your intentions are dishonorable, and you have not the spirit, as you have the aspect, of a gentleman, yet keep this secret, as you are a man."

"What shall be said to reassure you ?" demanded Montigny. "Witness, Heaven, if I assume to act, or intend anything injurious towards you. Believe me. I am the heir to a proud seigniory : you are,—I know not what ; enough for me to know, you are the fairest figure that has yet filled mine eyes, and surely as good as fair. Will you be mine, as I am yours for ever ? Speak, why are you silent ?"

"Hist," she said, listening.

"What is the matter ?" he enquired.

"Nothing, perhaps nothing :" she continued, whilst her voice faltered :—"but go, oh, go, and come again to-morrow, or next week, or when you will. I'll think on what you have said ; but go ; I tremble so ; stay here no longer ; think, should we be observed. I am ashamed to think of it. I am ashamed to look the moon in the face, ashamed to look into yours. Oh, sir, what have I done ? What have you said ? How have I answered ? for I am perplexed. Away, yet come again; come fifty times; but stay no longer now; begone;—return though when you choose; do not wait for an invitation.— Listen, I hear it again; begone, begone; did you not hear something?—it was nothing, perhaps, but yet begone."

"Never without your love pledge will I leave you," replied Montigny firmly.

"And would you force me to avow myself?" she asked. "May Heaven absolve me if I err herein! No, give me leisure to reflect: this were too sudden. These passion-hurried vows were too much like those vapors, that, igniting, rush like to unorbed stars across the night, then, vanished, leave it blacker. Do not tempt me. To act in haste is to repent at leisure; and quickliest lighted coals grow soonest cool. Even now I feel my cheek aglow with shame, that burns its passage to my rooted hair. Away: if you should not forget me, why, you are as though you were still present; for your thought, which is your truest self, remains with me. If you should grow oblivious—why, it is I that shall suffer, and not you."

"Oh, waste of words on what can never be!" exclaimed Montigny: "cease to doubt me. Forget you! Love's memories are immortal. Love writes the lineaments of the beloved in rock, not sand."

"Yet rocks may lose their effigies, the pyramids their inscriptions, the strong-clamped monument may tumble, and the marble bust, by time, may let the salient features fall into one indistinguishable round," she answered doubtingly.

"They may;" rejoined Montigny: "but neither

flowing time nor chafing circumstance can erase affection from the constant mind. Mind is more obdurate than steel; and love, the tenderest of the train of passions, is, in its memory, as indestructible as gold;—gold that resists the all-corroding fire. No; the fire may melt the impress from the seal, the sun the angles from the stony ice; the jagged rocks may from encounter with the wind and rain grow smooth; this hilly globe may grow at length to be as level as is the sea, and every jutting headland of the shore may crumble and disappear; but your bright image must to the eventide of life's cogitation, stay, like a sacred peak whose lofty brow stands ever gilded in the setting sun. Forget you! little hazard: he whose heart is impressed with the absent's form, needs wear no miniature upon the breast; the scholar who knows his task by rote, needs not retain his eye upon the book.

"Hearts may prove false," she answered solemnly, "and tasks to treacherous memory committed may be forgotten; but will you forget these weighty words: will you be constant, oh, will you prove true; for did I give you all I have, my love, what were there left me should you throw it away?"

"Injurious and incredulous one," returned Montigny, "save Lucifer, who ever threw from him heaven?"

"Forgive me," she replied, "it is but a timid girl that speaks. She did not doubt you, though she sought to prove you. Yet are you sure you love her? Ask your heart, then render me its reply, as one might do, who having listened for me to the murmuring shell, should bring me tidings of the storm-vexed sea. Vow not, but listen."

Montigny seemed for awhile to listen to his heart; then, looking at her, replied :

" Surer than is assurance itself I am yours. Say that you are mine, and every further word shall seem only to be redundant and apochryphal; for when love's lips have made their revelation, what more is wanting to complete the canon."

" Believe that I have said it," she half whispered; then, starting, and changing color, " hist, hist," she added, " once more I hear it: heard *you* nothing ? "

" I nothing heard but you." replied Montigny : " Proceed; for your voice is sweeter to me than plashing fountain's, or than Saint Laurent's chimes, or than would be—could we hear it—the fabulous music of those night-hung spheres, coming harmonious to our listening ears, borne on the shoulders of the cherub winds. Why are you silent ? "

" Listen," she said, looking still more alarmed.

" I do," he answered.

" Yet heard you nothing ? "

" Nothing but ourselves."

" Nothing besides ? "

" What further should I hear ? " he asked.

" And yet it seemed as if I heard another," she continued. " Are we watched ? speak, tell me," she demanded,—" I hear it again; listen."

Montigny listened a moment, then replied soothingly :

" Dismiss these pale-cheeked panics, for you hear nothing; or if you do it is but the common voices of the night. It is merely the hoarse bullfrog croaking in the swamp; and the green grasshopper a chirrupping in the meadow; for, saving these, all nature

with myself is listening to you. Be reassured : there
is nothing, but what your own excited fancy has
conjured : even the wind has ceased to sigh amongst
the leaves; the moon stands still, and her arrested
beam no longer draws the shadow on the dreamy
dial. Then, proceed, my love, for when you speak
you fill my ears with heaven, but when you pause
then opens the abyss."

"Yet listen; I hear it again:" she said; "it was
not fancy; no."

"What else? what can befall you, love, whilst I am
here?" he murmured.

"Nothing, I hope," she answered, falteringly.

"Then nothing dread."

"I dread to say it, yet I must: Good night."

"Already?" he demanded.

"All too long!" cried an imperious voice; and the
advocate stood before them.

"Amanda, ah, Amanda, Miss Macdonald," he continued, "is it thus you fool us? Go, bird, into your
cage. Nurse, take my lady in." And Amanda beheld
behind her the melancholy Mona, half shrouded in a
cloak covering her night attire.

Silently they both of them withdrew, and the
stranger was left alone with the advocate, who, lay-
ing his hand detectingly on the other's shoulder, thus
addressed him :

"Claude Montigny, I do not ask of you what brings
you here, for I have something overheard, and in
that something, all. Given the arc, the eye com-
pletes the perfect circle; furnished the angle and the
object's distance, and we can tell the dizzy altitude.
Mark me, sir. We climb with risk, but there is

" Amanda, oh! Amanda, is it thus you fool us?"

greater danger in descending. Young sir seigneur, you have ascended to a height you may not safely stoop from. As sportive and adventurous schoolboys sometimes ascend a scaffolding in the absence of the builders, and continue to scale from tier to tier, until they pause for breath; so, I fear, that you this night, in her protector's absence, have soared in the affections of my ward. Beware, beware: I would not threaten you—a gentleman neither needs nor brooks a threat—but, by my life and the strength that yet is left me, woe to the man that shall fool me in yonder girl! Seek not to trifle with me, Claude Montigny. Tell me your purpose; inform me how your acquaintance with my ward began; how it was fostered; how it has been concealed; and how it thus has ripened into this secret, midnight interview. Speak; what do you say, sir, in arrest of judgment? Be seated, and recount to me the story of your love, if you do love my ward—as you have told her that you do—and to that love be attached a story, long or brief; or if this passion—which you have propounded most passionately to her— be of a mere mushroom growth, born of to-night, sown by the hand of moonlight in a girl's dark eyes; or in her heart, perhaps, by the fairies that you spoke of, and producing some form of feeling or forced fruit of fancy; coeval with, and meant to be as transient, as is the present fungi of these fields. Sit down by me, and let your tongue a true deliverance make between yourself, me, and my foster-daughter." And seating himself heavily on a garden bench, and leaning with both hands clasped over the top of his gold-headed cane, he looked enquiringly up into the face of the young man, and added : " Come, plead before me to this charge of heart-stealing, as touching which you have been taken in the act."

" Sir," then said the stranger with dignity, whilst he slowly seated himself; " sir, you are justified in thus misdoubting me ; for though a gentleman should, like the wife of Cæsar, be above suspicion, never yet knew chivalry a time but there were recreant knights. Moreover, I can perceive that circumstances now must shadow, and, as with refracting influence, distort me, so that I may well stand here seeming to be deformed, although my soul, if you could see it, would show wanting no part of honour's fair proportions. Hear me, then, patiently, for I plead less for my own defence than for her vindication who has just retired beneath your frown."

And the ingenuous but compromised Montigny sketched the brief history of his passion, and when he had done, the advocate, looking into his countenance keenly, but confidingly, rejoined :

" You speak the truth, I know it by your eye, wherein no falsehood might harbour for a moment ; yet, young seigneur, you have entered on a perilous path ; dare you walk in it ? It is the way of honor, and will prove to be the way of safety ; but, beshrew me, if I do not fear that it may prove to you a way of pain. Whatever may be the ways of wisdom, the ways of honour are not always ways of pleasantness, nor is the path of duty always one of peace. If you would wear the rose you must grasp it as it grows amidst the thorns. And now, farewell—yet, hold. I hold you to your bond. The forfeit were the

forfeit of your word, which you have pledged to me
and mine. Remember, not only have you offered
love unto my ward, but you have been accepted."

"Even so :" exclaimed Montigny ; "and may—"

"Call nothing down that might become your
harm," said the advocate admonishingly : "Rain has
before now become transformed to hailstones, and
done much damage; and dews descending so benignly,
have once, it is said, in form of rain, swelled to a
deluge that has drowned the world. May the skies be
still propitious to you, Claude Montigny. Although
temptation burn as fiercely as dogdays, do not fall
beneath it, for less hurtful were a hundred sunstrokes
to the body, than to the soul is one temptation that
hath overcome it. Again farewell." And he pressed
Claude's hand convulsively, then tossed it from him
half disdainfully, and both departed from the grounds.

CHAPTER VIII.

"Think no more of this night's accidents."

Midsummer Night's Dream.

From Stillyside Claude Montigny rode towards the
western extremity of the island; his thoughts steeped
in bliss, and the country, as it slumbered in the
moonlight, seeming to him the land of Elysium. At
the ferry of Pointe Saint Claire he engaged a bateau
in which he was rowed over the confluence of the
rivers Ottawa and Saint Lawrence by four boatmen
who, from time to time, in a low tone, as if afraid
of awakening the dawn, chaunted, now an old song
of Normandy, and now a ballad upon the fate of some
lost voyageur. The moon was yet shining, and he
was in the mood to enjoy such minstrelsy; but when
they neared the opposite shore, a feeling of sadness
and apprehension stole over him, as he thought
of meeting his father, to whom he knew he must
either communicate distasteful tidings, or what was
worse to his ingenuous mind, practice a culpable concealment. Thus musing, as day broke he leaped on
shore, and again mounting his horse rode thoughtful
through forest and farm; now reburied in the darkness of night, which yet lingered amidst the foliage,
and now emerging into the light of the clearing; until, as the sun was rising over the opposite bank of
the St. Lawrence, he entered the manorial gates of

Mainville, and passing through the park-like grounds, was once more in the proud home of the Montignys.

Meantime, Amanda Macdonald had not slept. Shame, joy, fear, hope possessed her; but fear chiefly, for she dreaded the coming morrow, when she must meet her foster-mother, and—what to her was yet more terrible—her, as she supposed, deeply offended guardian; and it was not till the birds began to chirp and flit about her window, that she fell into a deep, refreshing slumber that lasted long into the day, and was at length broken by the voice of Mona bidding her arise.

The advocate, on the other hand, who had at once returned to town, arose at his usual hour, and repairing to his office, began the business of the day; whilst at a later period, the dissipated Narcisse again found his boon companions, and with them renewed the debauch of yesterday.

During the day the anxious Mona did not fail to question her charge touching the interrupted interview; and the latter at length related how it had befallen, confessed to her sudden passion for the gallant Montigny, revealed his plighted vows, and confiding herself to the bosom where she had always found advice and comfort, deprecated the displeasure of her guardian. But the betrayed Mona could give her only slight encouragement, in what was now yet nearer to her than even her guardian's favor, her lover's truth.

"Child," said Mona to her emphatically and in a warning tone, after musing, "Child, hope not too much; fear everything, for man is naturally false towards woman. All, you have yet learned but little

D

of man, and may you never learn too much.   Beware,
beware, beware, Amanda.   Happy the ignorant, happy is the woman whom no false man has taught
to distrust his sex !   Man's love to woman is as evan-
escent as is the presence of the summer-morning mist,
that, for an hour or so, hugs lovingly the lea, then
vanishes for ever.   What are his vows but vapour ?
Poor, rash girl, why, without warning me, have you
opened the horn-book of love, and spelled at such a
speed, that, in a day's time, you have read as far as
warier maids dare con in years ?"   And Amanda,
looked both abashed and amazed ; but at length
enquired in wonder :

"What may you mean by these strange utterances ?
Nay, nay, dear Mona : you slander your own father by
this language."

"Thou canst not say, child, that I slander thine,"
responded Mona, tartly ; and her countenance darkened with an equivocal expression new to Amanda, who,
catching at the inuendo, earnestly demanded,

"Who was my father ? tell me, for you know ; I
myself know, I feel, (and not untrustworthy is this
intuition) that I am not here a mere fortuitous
foundling.   Who was my mother ?   I charge you to
inform me."

"Girl, had not man been false, you had not needed
to have so often asked of me that question," Mona
replied with a cynical expression, and hoarse, sepul-
chral voice, that, whilst it seemed to vindicate herself, reproved her fellow, on whose face an air of horror now mantled, as she excitedly exclaimed :

"Say more, or else unsay what you have already
uttered.   What must be understood from this alarm-

ing language? Although there hangs a mystery over my birth, surely there rests upon it no dishonor. Acquaint me, then, once more I charge you, and now by the love and kindness that you have always shewn to me, declare, for you know—I say I feel you know; whose child am I, where was I born, how have I been committed to your care, adopted, cherished; I, who have no filial claims upon you; adjudged to be an orphan, perhaps the child of charity; how have I been divided between you and my guardian, or held as if I were your mutual bond? Inform me, Mona, my good Mona, foster-mother, nurse, you who have been to me as a true mother might be, say whose I am; whether, and where, my parents live; and, if they live, why they have thus abandoned me," and she burst into a flood of tears.

"Quiet yourself, my fond one," answered Mona, moved also to tears by this appeal; "your birth on one side is as high as any that this country boasts, therefore is as high as Claude Montigny's. Your mother is descended from a warlike Scottish line, your father's father was an English peer. Your parents are yet living; but their union, which was in many points unequal, was, alas! rendered the more unequal by a gulf-like disproportion in the passion that provoked it;—a gulf, too, that was undiscovered, till, too late, your mother saw it. Thence, their lives, their loves, so call it, their mutual progress (save on the course of fondness towards yourself, their child, whereon they journey equal side by side) has for years kept, and yet keeps, a still disparting pace; and, oh, Amanda, excuse these tears, for well I know your mother, and pity her, having many a time listened to her fruitless complaints; but until your father, who is the laggard one of this most mis-appointed pair, shall, either underneath the whip of a castigating conscience, or prompted by the spur of your poor mother's sharp appeals, come up abreast, and fill a certain chasm of omission by an indemnify-ing deed, which has been by him most selfishly left undone, but whose performance is essential to the full fruition by you of your fortune, you must remain, as you have hitherto done, my foster-child, and your grim guardian's ward; a waif we hold waiting for its claimants; and until they arrive, let me beseech you, as though I were the mother I have spoken of, to think no further of young Claude Montigny."

CHAPTER IX.

"Any bar, any cross, any impediment will be medicinable to me: I am sick in displeasure to him; and whatsoever comes athwart his affection, ranges evenly with mine. How canst thou cross this marriage?"

Much ado about nothing.

A few days after the conversation detailed in the preceding chapter, there was ushered into the office of the advocate at Montreal a gentleman, who announced himself as Montigny, Seigneur of Mainville. He was tall, and of a distinguished aspect, and had scarcely accepted of the advocate's invitation to be seated, when, like a man impatient to be done with a disagreeable business, he began :

" I have a son, sir, and you, as I believe, a ward, an orphan girl;" pronouncing with a mixture of pity and contempt the last two words.

The advocate observed this depreciatory intonation, and throwing himself backwards in his large easy chair, repeated : " An orphan girl," at the same time putting a half angry, half comical expression into his countenance, and perpetrating a pun in what followed : " Yes, many of your Canadian noblesse would bless themselves to have been her father. The poor fellow, it is well he is not here to have overheard you. An orphan girl : true, as you say, I have an orphan girl,— or one that passes for such ; a girl I love, a ward, a charming child, yonder at Stillyside. Were I disposed to praise her I might say she is the Mountain's maid ; the Dryad of its woods, a grace, a goddess,

fairer than Diana, and far purer, for one may guess
the fool Diana made of that poor boy, Endymion.
But what concerning my ward, sir, my most imma-
culate lady?"

"Would you forbid my son access to her?" enquired the seigneur.

"Ah! you wish for an injunction;" said the
advocate; "show me cause. I have, sir—as you
seem aware—a ward dwelling yonder at my seat at
Stillyside;—a place I sometimes visit; a sort of
shrine, a kind of hermitage or chapel, wherein two
devotees, two nun-like, holy women consume the
hours; leading there, pious, penitential lives, making
each day a sort of hallowed tide, and every eve a
vigil."

"You are humorous," replied the seigneur. "Excuse me, I am sorry, but it were best that I should
speak plainly. I would not wish to see your ward
dishonored."

"Dishonored! not a seigneur, nor a seigneur's son
dare dream of such a consummation, nor, daring so to
dream, could compass it," cried the advocate, growing
crimson. "Yet this is kind of you;" he added,
bowing as if deeply grateful;—" and yet," he continued, "there can be no fear of an offence : is not
your son a clergyman? for, if he be, and they confess
to him anything worse than to have admitted him to
their confidence—why, sir, he shall be allowed to
enter, and shrive them when he chooses;" and after
a momentary silence, "Fie! fie!" he resumed, roll-
ing in his chair; "'the fool hath said in his heart
there is no God,' and the wise man of Mainville,
who has been all his life looking for purity in a

petticoat, says 'there is no virtue in woman.' But
I say, both these oracles are in the wrong; there is
not only a Divinity, but there are women too who
are virtuous. This is a clumsy jest, sir. My ward
be dishonored by your son? Yes, when the diamond
can be cut with a feather. Monsieur Montigny, a
tempest is as harmless as a breath, when that tempest
is being hurled against the rock; a breath is even as
effectual as is a tempest, when that breath is puffed
against the dust. So buzzing blandishments of sigh-
ing fops, may blow the frail flowerets from weak,
wanton natures; whilst vehement vows of otherwise
most honorable men, though urged as strongly as the
northern blast, are in vain against the marble front
of virtue. I am marble to your wishes."

"You weigh your danger as little as you do your
language," observed the seigneur. "Will you permit a trespasser, a tempter within your grounds; a
wolf, a fox, a bear within your fold?"

The advocate shrugged his shoulders and replied:
" No, heaven forbid ;—and Stillyside is to me as an
outer court of heaven, wherein my ward dwells as a
sort of semi-solitary angel."

"Yet angels fell, and so may she fall," interjected
the seigneur quickly.

"They did, and without a tempter, too, Monsieur
Montigny," returned the advocate, quietly; then
added : "the height of heaven turned the heads of the
angels giddy."

"Girls are giddy," remarked the seigneur gravely.

"Boys are more frequently foolish," drily retorted
the advocate : "and often coming to girls for kisses, go
away with cuffs. I hope your son has neither sought

for the one nor yet received the other. But what is
this son, Monsieur Montigny, that you would have
me believe to be so formidable? Is he another Lucifer, couched at my ward's ear, as his dark prototype
once squatted at that of Eve? Or is he Lothario alive
again? Is he Leander, and are the Ottawa's jaws a
western Hellespont, with my ward and Stillyside, for
Hero and her tower?"

" Your verandah," remarked the seigneur, " is not
higher than was Hero's tower, although, I trust, your
ward's virtue may be more exalted than was Hero's.
But are you aware, sir, that already my son has had
her company, alone, at midnight, on your grounds;
all others retired; she alone watching, with Claude
Montigny and the broad, full moon?"

" An actionable moon," exclaimed the lawyer, " and
a decided case of lunacy against the lovers. But,
alas, sir, in this respect we have all been sinners in
our youth, and all grown wondrous righteous with
our years. Have we not ourselves, when we were
young,—ay, and upon inclement winter nights too,
courted brown peasant girls beneath both stars and
moon? What if the nights were cold, the blood was
warm; and now with these volcanic veins of ours
grown cool, why, we may walk on the quenched crater
of concupiscence, and who dares challenge us, and say,
ha, ha! smut clings to you, gentlemen; you have
the smell of fire upon you. No, sir, no; we are fu-
migated, ventilated, scented, powdered, purged as with
hyssop. Pish! he must be truly an Ethiop, whom
time cannot whiten; a very leopard, who will not
part with his spots, since the sun himself shall lose
his some day, purged in his own fires."

" I repeat, sir, your ward is in danger," said the
seigneur doggedly.

" Not at all. Is the diamond in danger when it is
put into the crucible ; is the gold deteriorated when
it is being deterged from dross ?" was responded.

" Infatuated man., would you open the door to the
seducer ?" asked the seigneur, growing angry with
the contumelious lawyer.

" Seducer !" said the advocate, affecting to be
shocked : " that is a huge stone to throw at your own
son : and remember ; is not every man's frame a glass
house, whereat the soul that inhabits it should invite
no stone throwing from the little red catapult of a
neighbour's tongue ?   Beware, beware; have mercy,
Monsieur Montigny.   ' All flesh is grass,' the Pro-
phet proclaims ; but I assert, ' All flesh is glass.' "

" A woman's reputation is as brittle," was the
seigneur's ready repartee ; " therefore warn off my son
from Stillyside."

" But should he not regard me, sir, what then ?"

" Brandish the law over him, your chosen weapon,"
answered the seigneur.

The lawyer suddenly looked grave, and, affecting to
be offended, demanded sternly : " Monsieur Montigny,
am I a mere mechanic to do your bidding ?   Brandish
the law indeed !   Is, then, the law but an ordinary
cudgel, to thwack the shoulders with or beat the
brains out ?   The law, sir, is a sacred weapon, not to
be lightly taken up, neither to be profanely applied
to paltry uses, any more than we would take the
tempered razor to pick a bone, or pare our cheese
with.   Brandish the law !   The man that can talk
of brandishing the law would brandish a piece of the

true cross, sir, if he had it; he would drink, sir, from his mother's skull, and with his father's thigh-bones play at shinty. What is the law? What less is it than the will and force of all employed for one; the savage sense of justice, disciplined and drilled till it can move in regular array, invincibly, to conquer wrong; surely too vast an engine to be employed on trifles. Who wants a wheel to break a butterfly upon; or, to crush a worm who calls for a pavior's rammer? Monsieur Montigny, listen. Mercy is Heaven's first attribute, and the executioner is the State's meanest, as well as last, servant; shall I, then, stoop to this, who may aspire to that? Shall I wield a whip of legal scorpions before your son, should he seek to re-enter Stillyside? Would you have me, as once Heaven's cherubim stood at the gates of Paradise, with fiery swords turning all ways, to hinder its ejected tenants from breaking back into the garden,—would you have me, I say, stand at my gates at Stillyside, and, meeting young Montigny, flourish in his face a fist full of fasces, in the form of threatened pains and penalties? No; your suit, sir, is denied: you take nothing by your motion."

"Dare you deny," retorted the seigneur, loudly, and with a look of coming triumph; "dare you deny that you are privy to their intimacy; will you assert that you—yourself unseen—have not witnessed my son in secret, midnight conversation with your ward at Stillyside; there overheard them interchanging vows of endless love, and dealing declarations of devoted-ness unto each other;—I ask you; did you not hear and see these doings, and, even when you did at length surprise the pair, did you not by failing to condemn their folly, give it your silent sanction?"

" Something of this I did," said the advocate
coolly, " for I remembered some rather liberal
breathings of my own when I was young,—and
youth will have its fling,—nay, do not bite your lip,
but listen. Monsieur Montigny, thus far we have met
guile with guile. Just like two wily fencers, both of
us, waiting to spy our advantage, have still witheld
the lunge, until, at last, you, having grown desperate,
have rushed into the close. Yet, do not let your
anger overbear discretion. The heated iron hisses
when it is plunged into the trough, but shall we hiss
at each other like geese or serpents? Shall we quarrel,
deny the undeniable, try to undo the accomplised
deed? What is done is done, and not Omnipotence
itself, sir, could undo it."

" But we may hinder further evil," observed the
seigneur.

" Ay? Would you keep out the lightning by
high builded walls?" demanded the advocate, " for
you are as likely to accomplish that, as to keep
lovers from each other. No, let them alone, for they
are as climbing Titans towards their wishes' skies;
despising guardians' gates and fathers' fences, just as
much as did Briareus and his crew disdain its rugged
sides, and risk their necks up steep Olympus, when
they were making war on Jove. You cannot bar
them. The sun may be debarred from attics, and frost
may be kept out of cellars, but, Monsieur Montigny,
the mutually enamoured can never be permanently
parted. Sir, no more."

" Enamoured he, and she at length dishonoured,"
cried the seigneur, disregarding the injunction.

" Her honour is its own sufficient guardian," was
responded.

" Have regard, sir, to your future peace," was urged.

" Peace, sir, like silence, never comes for calling for," rejoined the advocate.

" Impracticable man, have you no fear ?" demanded the foiled Montigny upbraidingly.

" None for my ward; I hope you have as little for your son," said the lawyer sarcastically.

" Your ward invites my son, by sitting upon the verandah at midnight, to attract him when he passes by, as the Hebrew woman, Tamar, once sat to decoy the foolish Judah. Do you deny this ? I have learned all, all," outburst the indignant seigneur.

" Do I deny it ?" cried the advocate, the blood, in anger, rushing to his face. " Dare you affirm it ? Monsieur, if you mean seriously to asperse my ward, I say, prepare ;—not for the action of the law,—no, no, I hate the law, when it is cited for myself,—but for the action of an old man's arm. Sir, I have been a swordsman in my youth, and though the lank ske- leton of my skill at fence is buried in disuse, it moves now in the grave of this right hand, that so long has wielded only the quiet quill. I do not bid you quail ; not I,—but, by the angry devil of the duel, you answer me, either sword point to sword point ; or from the pointing pistol, that shall speak both sharp and decisive, and the dotting bullet, perhaps, put a period to your proud life's scrawl. But no ; I am grown too old to have recourse to violence. Away, go, go ; but, mind you, do not breathe this calumny into a human ear,—no, not into the air. Shame, shame ! you are no noble minded man, to villify my ward and your own son ; whom, if I accounted to be as strangely base as you have shown yourself to be, and have depicted him, I would forbid to tread within my gates, and hound him from my door at Stillyside."

" Words only anger you," said the astonished and half daunted seigneur.

" Such words as yours have been:" was replied. " What! do you expect to strike upon a bank where bees have settled, yet not be stung; or dream to be allowed to draw the bare hand, clasping down a sword, but not be wounded?"

" What shall I say, yet not offend you?" soothingly enquired Montigny.

" Say what you will," the advocate continued: " what can be worse than what you have said already?"

" Hear me," said the seigneur, in the manner of one who is going to make a confidential proposal: " Either remove your ward, and receive a compensation for her absence, or quickly marry her, and I will provide her with a dower."

" Now you are indeed a generous gentleman," said the advocate, smiling; " You must have built churches, surely, or founded hospitals, and always have dealt out dollars liberally to the deserving. But you are wealthy, and can do these things without being impoverished. It is fortunate that you are wealthy, for I shall accept of no paltry sum. Only imagine, to have to banish her; to quench, or to remove, the very beam that fills my life with light. You must be liberal, if you would have me exile her Come, sign me a bond for what I shall demand."

" You are in haste," observed the seigneur, somewhat startled at the advocate catching so readily at the bait; but the latter was ready with his reply:

" Because your son may now be at Stillyside, and, whilst we are haggling, may carry off my ward,—or I might change my mind," he answered.

" And I, too, may change mine," was the rejoinder.

" Why, then, we are quits;" observed the advocate carelessly, and as if all parley were at an end; " we are as we were, and, for the young ones, they are as they were; but if I know the force of youthful blood, you, with all your endeavours, will not be able long to keep them apart."

" What is your price for her expatriation ?" demanded the seigneur sullenly, as if coming to terms ; and the advocate replied :

" No, marry her, marry her; we will have her married. We either marry her or do nothing in this business, sir, which, after all, were, perhaps, best left to those who have most interest in it;—but if you think differently, be it yours to find the money, I will find the match :—and let it be understood, that you find her a dowry which would be fitting for a seigneur's daughter; or else, without a dowry, I shall not scruple to give her to a seigneur's son. Why are you silent ?"

The proud, perplexed parent made no answer, but secretly groaned in his dilemma, and at length exclaimed : " Insatiate old man, have you no son, the thought of which may teach you to be just towards me and mine ? What do I ask of you ? Little ,—or what would cost you little, yet you ask a fortune of me; and to enrich, too, one, whom, as a punishment, I have reason rather to desire should always be poor. Do not deny it; she has ensnared my son. It is impossible, that he who has roamed over half the world, and has yet come home uncaptivated, though in his travels he has met the fairest and the richest, can have been caught at the mere passing by your farm of Stillyside, can at a glance have been so smitten as to meditate this marriage. No, he has been decoyed, seduced. You might as well declare that a young eagle would not return to its nest, but plunge into some casually discovered coop, and roost there, as aver that, without some irregular influence, Claude Montigny would seek your ward in marriage. If she marry him, she will marry a beggar: not an acre of mine shall he inherit, not a dollar of mine will he receive. Give her a dowry? Give her a dukedom. No, sir; I will not buy brass from you at the price of gold; I will not subsidize you to avoid your ward." And, with the words, he bowed himself out of the room, and the advocate, casting himself backwards in his easy chair, laughing, exclaimed: " Was ever such a proposition started?—started! yes; and shall eventually be carried. It is not what we do, but it is the motive that induced the deed, that gives the color to it. She shall be Madam Montigny, in spite of old Montigny's self; and for her dowry, (which I asked Montigny to provide, only that it might be returned to him through his son), I'll mortgage my old brains to procure it for her."

CHAPTER X.

While you here do snoring lie
Open-ey'd conspiracy
His time doth t.ke:
If of life you keep a care,
Shake off slumber, and beware:
Awake! Awake!

The Tempest.

Amongst the seigniories contiguous to the eastern extremity of the island of Montreal, lies that of Montbœuf. Its present owner was André Duchatel, a descendent of the Sieur Duchatel, a cadet of an ancient French noble family, to whom the seigniory was granted by royal letters patent, about the middle of the seventeenth century. But if any nobility of soul, or refinement of aspect existed in the first of the Canadian dynasty of Duchatel, it had not been transmitted to the living representative of the line. As the long hung-up sword or unused ploughshare, lose their brightness and edge from want of use, perhaps these qualities of mind and body had disappeared for want of a fitter field for their display. André Duchatel, seigneur of Montbœuf, was a vulgar looking, short, broad-set, florid figure, of fifty years or so; material in his tastes, in disposition obstinate and narrow-minded, unenlarged by education; shy with strangers, yet fond of good fellowship with his acquaintance, and, with much reason, accounted to be rich. He was a widower, but lived

in a kind of surly, patriarchal state, in the midst of
three sons and a daughter; the former being dissipated and sensual, the latter of a showy person, but
in character, superficial, vain, vindictive, proud.

An intimacy had long existed between the houses
of Montigny and Duchatel, which, in spite of their
different genius, had for generations continued as it
were to shake hands across the island. The latter
family, though equal to the former in wealth and
pedigree, secretly acknowledged it as the superior,
and with a view to an alliance between the two,
Seraphine Duchatel, even when a child, was a fre-
quent visitor at Mainville; her relations hoping that
thereby, she and Claude Montigny might become
inspired with a mutual liking, the prelude to their
desired union.

This union, it was understood, was to be cemented
on the part of Duchatel, by the gift, as her marriage
portion, of a tract of land adjoining the seigniory of
Mainville, and at present the property of André
Duchatel; but which, at the nuptials, would be
added to the Montigny manor, as a sort of arrière
fief, and so gratify the craving of the elder Montigny
for territorial aggrandizement. The splendid person
of Claude had long ago caught the slight affections
of Seraphine, who in her visits to Mainville, would
hang upon him, much to his distaste, and persist to
make him her reluctant cavalier, though neither her
blandishments nor his father's wishes could induce
him to return these visits, or appear to reciprocate
her preference. Nor would a closer and wider
acquaintance with the Duchatels have lessened his
reluctance. The eldest son, Samson, was a colossal

E

bully, dividing his time between field sports, intemperance, and intrigues with the daughters of the censitors on his father's seigniory; or in yet lower illicit amours with the peasant girls of the manorial village; varied by occasional journeys, made more for debauchery than business, to the city of Montreal. The second scion of the house, Pierre, was a goodenough looking, and not ill-disposed youth; whom his father, as if willing to offer up his choicest lamb for the sins of the family fold, had intended for the church. But the former had far other intentions towards the fair than absolving them from their peccadilloes, and entertained other ideas of foreign travel than that of going on distant Indian missions; whilst the youngest brother, Alphonse, was an unbroken colt and madcap, articled to one of the principal legal firms in the city. Although in years he was but ancle deep, he was already in potations full five fathoms; a worthy graduate of the licentiousness of the town, and boon companion of the dissolute Narcisse; whom, in a giddy moment he had made acquainted with the family matrimonial design on young Montigny. Narcisse, in his turn, had a domestic story, that instinct, revenge, and a mother's command impelled him to relate, and which he told to the rollicking, but now attentive Alphonse, with a wicked glee, raised by the prospect of mischief. A discovery had been made by his brooding and despised parent. Chance had thrown in her way an opportunity for which she had watched for years. Mona Macdonald had visited the advocate at his dwelling, and her presence had stirred not only the womanly curiosity of the lynx-eyed Babet Blais, but her malicious jealousy of one whom she could never but regard as a hateful and favored rival. So, overhearing them in earnest conversation in the library, she, with the unrestrained enjoyment of a low, untutored nature, stole to the door, that was slightly ajar, and there, with her ear applied to the interstice, learned the circumstance of the discovered interview between Claude and Amanda at Stillyside, with their plighted troth, not disapproved of by the advocate. Swelling with envy and anger, and recollecting what Narcisse had told her of the predilection and hopes of Alphonse Duchatel's sister in regard to Claude Montigny, she, with an intent to dash the proud prospect which seemed to be opening before the child of an odious—and as she deemed, unlawful competitor for the advocate's favors, conceived the spiteful idea of informing the Duchatels of what she had just discovered. Further to instigate her, all the real and all the fancied wrongs that her son had suffered from his father rose up before her, magnified by her imagination, and prompting her to the gratification of her unreasoning spleen. Her purpose was soon put into execution. That night Narcisse came home sober; and giving him some warm supper, followed by a delicacy that she had set aside for him as a dessert, and which, with a half human, half animal affection, she watched him devour, she broke the subject to him. He grinned with an infantile delight, as he heard the important secret, and discussed with her the project that might hinder the good fortune of the haughty foundling, whose disdain had long chagrined him, and under the recollection of whose scorn during the recent raid on Stillyside, he was yet smarting. With heightened pleasure she beheld his joyful interest, and, warming with his sympathy, whilst she gloated over the anticipated revenge, she exclaimed, as her face assumed a dark, prophetic aspect : "Yes, we will humble that mongrel, and her proud, petted child. What better are they than we, what nearer to thy father ? See how I toil, and do his drudgery ; keep him a home, who, but for me, would have no home, and no one to care for him. Yet no fine country house for me, fine clothes, rich presents ; no fine gifts for thee, my child, no endless schooling, no sending *thee* to travel ; no allowance, no expense to help to make of thee a gentleman, like his endeavours to make her child a lady ; no fine lady sought for thee to be thy wife, Narcisse ; no closetings for me, who, but for her, had been thy father's wife, and not his servant. But God and the virgin have at last heard our prayers. Narcisse, my darling, tell Alphonse Duchatel all that I have told thyself. Bid him quickly inform his father, brothers, sister ; and if they have French blood in their veins they will balk this half-breed and her daughter brat."

Never was there an apter pupil than Narcisse proved now ; never a willinger. Scarcely could he refrain from at once rushing forth to find his friend, Alphonse ; and he did at length arise with the blessing and Godspeed of his mother, intending to inform him, touching the rival who had so far and so suddenly outstripped his sister on the road of Claude's regard, when the voice of the advocate was heard calling upon his son to attend him in the room above. Narcisse obeyed ; but filled with a sentiment of rising rebellion and new-born insolence, as of one who intends no longer to be checked, nor submit to unmerited harshness and tyranny. There the two had an altercation, provoked by the old grudges, and aggravated by Narcisse's recent dissipation, escapade, and neglect of duty, and still more sharpened by his present pertness and contumacy. Anger rose high between parent and child, and the latter, in unconcealed dudgeon flung from the room, and left the house, his breast charged with a spiteful purpose; and going straight to the lodgings of Alphonse Duchatel, he told all—and more than all—that he had learned respecting the menaced alliance between the children of Mainville and Montbœuf.

Burning with the information, the young and impetuous Alphonse scarcely slept that night, and in the morning, having obtained leave of absence, rode swiftly to his paternal home, and, in sudden, solemn family council, declared what he had learned of danger to the connubial scheme that had long been planned for his sister and the distinction of their house.

CHAPTER XI.

" Then hie you hence to Friar Laurence' cell."
Romeo and Juliet.

" Given to captivity me and my utmost hopes."
Othello.

Whilst the news that Claude Montigny had given, to a girl of dubious birth and uncertain social position, the heart, for the possession of which the supercillious Seraphine Duchatel had so long striven in vain, was disturbing the souls of the Montbœuf Manorhouse, the seigneur of Mainville, ill at ease, and apprehensive of a hasty and irremediable matrimonial step on the part of his son, started for Montreal again to visit the intractable advocate.

Later in the same day, Claude also took horse, and rode towards the banks of the Ottawa, where he arrived at dusk, and crossing at the ferry from the main to Sainte Anne, he thence, solitary, and filled with chequered thoughts, continued his way, whilst the ground grew dimmer and yet dimmer, and star after star stole out; till, as the moon rose slowly in the glimmering air, he reached the neighbourhood of dim Mount Royal.

At the same hour that the large bateau was heaving its way over the vexed flood of the meeting waters of the Saint Lawrence and the Ottawa, four horsemen crossed a rustic bridge, that led from the mainland to the opposite, or eastern extremity of the

Island of Montreal. One of the riders was of gigantic stature, and another of diminutive proportions; and all were clad in the coarse grey frieze suit of the country, and wore upon their heads the common blue cap or tuque. Pursuing their way, they kept to the least frequented paths; endeavouring to avoid recognition; until the coming night concealed them, and they journeyed beneath the decrescent and feebly shining moon.

And now, whilst such was transpiring at the extremities of the Island, at Stillyside, its centre, the curtains had been drawn, and the lighted lamp, with its frosted glass globe, shone serene and silvery, like a minor and domestic moon. Mona Macdonald sat sewing near a table, whilst Amanda read aloud. On a sofa a lazy lapdog dreamed, the parrot slept on its swing, and the bullfinch on the perch in its cage, and in the pauses of Amanda's voice, the drowsy cat was heard purring in its evening doze. Nothing was heard without, except the fitful bark of the New-foundland dog at some stray passer by; and, at length, even that had ceased; Mona's needle was laid aside, the domestics, obedient to the early habits of country life, were abed, Mona herself had now retired, and Amanda being left alone, nothing was heard but the measured ticking of the old clock on the corner of the stairs. The lamp had been taken away by the departing Mona, and in the obscurity, the moonbeams fell in grey streaks adown the damask curtains; and after a brief meditation on the subject of her reading, Amanda rose, noiselessly ascended the carpeted stairs to her room, approached the window, drew aside the drapery, and gazed towards Mainville.

Thus had she done each night since the memorable interview with Claude Montigny; and now not less long did she linger there, but longer; nor thought of retiring, till, startled at the approaching sound of horses, she hastily re-closed the curtains; the sound ceased, and she began slowly to undress. But her thoughts were elsewhere; and, falling into a reverie, she sat with her raised fingers still upon her dress, that she was about to withdraw from before her snowy bosom, when again she heard the sound of hoofs on the road, and soon a shaking of reins near the gate, and champing of the bit, mingled with the smothered growl of the awakened Newfoundlander. Divining the cause, and seized with trembling, she arose, again threw aside the curtains, and beheld in the moonlight a figure advancing up the lawn. A moment she gazed upon the apparition; then, scarcely knowing what she did, opened the folding window, and half within and half without her chamber, leaning forward into the night, demanded in a piercing whisper of enquiry and alarm: " Who comes there ? Speak, is it Claude Montigny ?"

" It is I, my love, for by what name shall you be called, yet dearer, worthier than love ?" responded the subdued, yet full, clear voice of Claude. Then, drawing nearer, he continued in an enraptured tone:

" Oh, my lady, oh, my heart, my love, my life; my mistress now, my wife that is to be: my breath, my soul; my hope, my happiness, my all in all; fair presence—but in vain my tongue seeks for the word that shall embody you, and, like the hunted hare returning to its form, so does my soul return to that word, love. My love, then, be it, for you are my love, you are my life henceforward; nor shall the hereafter part us, for wherever you are there unto me will still be heaven. Oh, my love, is it not kind of fortune thus to call you forth? a favorable omen of the issue of this night. Oh, come forth, my love; come forth, and make a hallowed aisle of the verandah."

"Alas!" exclaimed Amanda, stepping to the verandah, "why have you ventured here again so soon,—or, rather, why so late? for are there not ruffian robbers on the road, and all the secret perils of the night?"

"No peril equals that of absence from yourself," said Claude, "for passion has greater perils than the road. Cupid's arrows are more terrible to him whose breast is bared by the absence of its mistress, than would be at the traveller's throat the armed and threatening hands of fifty ruthless robbers. But how have you fared since we were so rudely parted?"

Amanda sighed. "But so so;" she murmured mournfully, "it is a slight burn that does not smart a little when the scorched part is snatched away from the fire:" and hanging down her head bashfully, repeated, "But so so:—I have felt an unaccustomed care—of little consequence,—but, oh, tell me, Montigny, how your father, the proud, rich seigneur takes this matter, for I know you would inform him of it. Is he not incensed, not angry; does he not upbraid you, and call me evil, and perhaps deserved, hard names?"

"He has expostulated with me; Claude responded; "yet not with too much earnestness, knowing love's fires are blown by opposition. How seems your guardian?"

"How shall I dare to meet him!" murmured Amanda musing.

" Do not fear him ;" Claude rejoined : " he will not chide you;—besides, you shall be gone to-morrow. I come to-night, a Jason for the golden fleece, and may not return without it. Stillyside is Colchis, and my desires are dolphins that have brought me hither, and will not, returning, ferry me across the Ottawa, unless they shall be freighted with your form. Mine own one, do not stand transfixed like death in life, but live here no longer; leave it, and live with me for ever, for from where you are my feet shall never stray. Do not misdoubt me : though man were as faithless as it is said that woman is fickle, yet I were loyal towards *you*, whom I implore to be my affianced to-night, my bride to-morrow."

" To-morrow !—Oh, so soon," exclaimed Amanda, starting.

" It will be a thousand years till then ;" interposed Montigny; "and yet it will be the glad millenium, since you shall reign amidst my meditations, and towards you all my thoughts be worshipping saints. This dumb devotion will be bliss, but to have sealed you mine by the great sacrament of marriage will be glory, such as the saved soul experiences when, in Heaven sitting, it feels itself secure, and proof against the possibility of loss. Accord me your consent. Why do you ponder ? wherefore should you hesitate ? Amanda, be immediately mine. What are your thoughts ? What are you that transports me with impatience out of myself, to mingle with your being, and become one with yourself in history and fate ? Our fate commands; let us obey it, since, what is fate's behest, but Heaven's directing voice; what is our destiny, but the deed which we perceive may not be left undone."

"Rash man, forbear;" pronounced Amanda, her face darkening with displeasure; "you counsel me to evil. Though I would esteem you as I would some annunciating angel, beyond impeachment of veracity, and bent on a generous errand, you seem as a fallen spirit now; tempting me, not enlightening. No, Montigny, no. Shall I deceive my guardian so kind, shall I defraud your house, your father, you? I, who have no fortune, nor—as is your lot—upon my name, neither the rime and hoar of silver, new renown, nor golden rust of brown antiquity,—the dust of ages in heroic deeds, lying on your escutcheon, dyeing it as the dust that dapples the bright insect's wings;—shall I, I say, come and lie like to a bar sinister across it? for what else should I be considered by your indignant friends, except, indeed, a shadow on your brightness, a shame across your honour?" and she hung her head in despairing sadness, whilst Montigny thus replied:

"Oh, shame on me, to hear you so self-slandered! Friends! mistaken friends. And what although my father and the world esteemed you my inferior; what were their estimation unto me; and, compared with you, what is the value of heraldic honours and traditionary glory heaped upon the dead, which is, in truth, too often only as the phosphorescent glimmer that hangs upon decay: what are these gauds to me, who count you to be far above the worth of monumental effigy, or marble mask, my living love; whom I will set,—not in the tomb of cold, pale

porphyry, nor in a sable, slabbed sarcophagus, but
breathing, and enshrined in fortune's framing gold.
Fastidious girl, and prouder than the proud Montignys, listen to me, listen. We are two stranger
vessels that have met upon the highway of the
lonely sea;—we are as two ships that, being long
from port, have, sailing, met, and exchanged one
with the other, what each has needed and what each
could spare; we have bartered heart for heart. Have
you not given me yours? If you have not, why,
then, return me mine."

"Then were I poor indeed," replied Amanda.

"Yet I were poorer without yours," retorted
Claude, "poorer than he who begs his bread. I wish
I had to beg my bread for you, then richly should
you fare; for who, when I should crave for love of
you, (as mendicants ask alms for love of heaven),
could then refuse me? Oh, refuse no longer my
request. Estimate not my fortune, but appraise
myself; and whatsoever you may deem to be my
value, account your own worth as being ten thousand times that sum. Still take me, a mere miserable
doit; an earnest, an instalment towards the payment
of the debt of love and loyalty, that shall require a
life to liquidate, then leave me bankrupt in untold
arrears."

" I should forgive the debt, even before you could
have asked forgiveness," replied Amanda, smiling,
though much moved; "and yet I would not leave
you perfectly absolved, but still retain you by some
small reminder, some power of execution over you—
not to be exercised towards you to your hurt—far
from it, but I would be absolute that I might shew you

mercy; even as noblest kings have been despotic, and
in their day have delighted in dispensing pardon.
So would I be towards you;—or even as the King of
Kings—to speak it reverently—who, of His bound-
less goodness and free grace, remits the debts and
manifold trespasses of us, his poor, defaulting
creatures."

"Go on, for it is bliss to hear you," murmured
Claude.

"Nay, I have done;—what have I said?" she
quietly enquired of him.

"Would you unsay it?" he demanded eagerly.

"Only to say it again," she answered blushing,—
" yet I fear I have babbled strangely;—but, remember, I was never wooed before, nor answered wooer;
so, being a novice in love's archery, it may be that
the gust of a too ardent breath has caught my words,
and from my meaning wafted them awry."

"And can a fountain yield both bitter and sweet?"
demanded Claude: " or are you as changeful as is yon
waning moon?" he asked half chidingly.

"Rather consider me to be as is the sun, that knows
no change of aspect throughout the livelong year;
or, if it vary, swells its orb in winter," she observed,
"even as I would now appear to you with fuller
favor, amidst this young acquaintance's chilly prospect."

"Chilly! it is summer wherever lovers cast their
eyes, the bright Bermudas. Do not libel love, nor
our sweet fortunes," cried Claude impetuously: "For
me, there never will be winter where you are; and
why, when I am with you, should you thus seem
to shiver, as it were, in the shadow of November?"

"I am no casuist," she said, "and yet it would appear to be too selfish in me, too much like to fraud, should I accept all that you offer me, such vast and personal advantage, and for which I bring you no equivalent, no dower, no estate; nothing to counterpoise the wide possessions that you will inherit;—nothing that may conciliate your family, rich in material things and heaped with honors,—save my poor love;—and what were that?"

"More than them all," ejaculated Claude, "but why these scruples? In human hearts love is not placed against love, as in the scales the commodity is placed against the weight; neither is it exchanged for land, or bartered for position; but it is always given, and is the donor's whole, unmeasured and immeasurable. It is infinite, growing whilst it is being given, even as the horizon grows upon the eye of him who travels towards it. It *is* because *it must* be; it is unselfish; nay, unto itself it is unjust; often giving the most where it receives the least; possessing nothing, yet possessing all, if it possesses but all its object's heart. It is towards its object as is the encircling and cloud-breeding sea unto the verdant island, encompassing, and in soft showers, shedding itself over it. As the sea sheds itself in soft showers upon the island, so do I shed my fondness, and would shed my fortune, over you, and in return seek for yourself,—no more, for what more could you give, what more could I receive, who count all else as worthless dross. What hinders then our marriage?"

"Your father," was replied.

"He would not consent unto our nuptials though I should pray him on my bended knees, so obstinate and unyielding is his pride," asseverated Claude.

"My guardian, too, is proud," answered Amanda.

"Let us not wait, but wed without, and not against their leave, then;" Montigny urged adroitly :—"but your guardian will consent: he has avowed as much unto me privately; so, mark; when morning brings the daylight to the east, be ready. Meet me beyond these grounds; when we will hasten to the village of Saint Laurent, and there be married. The deed being thus achieved, none will oppose, for before the irrevocable all rebuke is dumb."

"And so am I to this," was replied with dignity.

"Yet let me speak:" Montigny urged with desperate eagerness, "let me persuade you, for to this pass it must come; then let it come at once, since each day will cause the path thereunto to grow more rugged. My father's storm of threats, my mother's deluge of tears, will make the way impassable and past repair. You falter; your silence speaks consent; you are convinced, and yield to the necessity for this ungracious consummation. Good night. To-morrow early, meet me at the church of Saint Laurent, all shall be ready,—pray offer no remonstrance;—meet me there at ten,—the priest is my fast friend;—nay, do not grieve, but say good night; to-morrow you shall smile :—good night, good night;" and kissing his hand to her, before she could reply, the impetuous lover reached the postern, and, vaulting into the saddle, vanished.

Paralyzed with amazement and apprehension, Amanda stood motionless and dumb. She would have called on Claude to return, but dare not, lest she should alarm the slumbering inmates of the house, and she was still standing irresolute and

helpless, when something was suddenly thrown over
her face, shrouding her in darkness, and before she
could resist she was lifted from her feet, hurried
across the lawn in a diverse direction from that
taken by Claude, and on arriving on the road, swung
into a lofty saddle. A huge arm from some one seated
behind received her, passing around her waist, and
feeling like the coil of a boa-constrictor ; and, amidst
the sound of several persons mounting in haste, spurs
were struck into the sides of the large animal, that
reared with a vast bound which nearly dismounted
its riders ; and at once, as it seemed, a troop were
flying with her at the top of their speed along the
road. Half fainting from terror, and stifling in the
folds of some coarse envelopment, she was unable to
utter a cry for help, and the cavalcade scoured along
its way. One seemed to ride before them, and the
rest behind. No one spoke, but her companion on the
crupper grasped her tightly, like a relentless fate, and
onwards they still bounded, and the deeply spurred
steeds in agony of exertion stretched themselves to
the task, and still they flew, and still Amanda strove
to recover her voice ; till as the dumb, in some
moment of mortal terror, are said to have found speech,
she, with accents, that, bursting through the thick veil,
rung amidst the night, shrieked out the name of
Claude Montigny. A low, chuckling laugh arose
around her, followed by a curse, and a hoarse threat
of violence from the figure that rode on the crupper,
who at the same time again dug spurs into the
flanks of the courser, that once more, with its huge,
responding bound nearly dismounted its riders ; and
prompted as it seemed by fear of a rescue, the rate

"The party tore along the road, shaking it as the prairie is shaken when it is swept over by a herd of buffaloes."

accelerated till the troop was scouring over the ground with the flight of a tempest. Confused with terror, and alarmed at the threats of her powerful keeper, she remained silent, unable to divine in what direction they were hurrying; but felt that her captor and custodian kept looking behind, as if afraid of some one in pursuit; and the killing pace appeared to rise yet higher, and the animals to quiver in quick bounds like mortal throes, as the spurs were plied up to the rowels, and the creatures seemed to swallow the ground, until again over all burst, as might the shriek of an imprisoned gnome, from beneath her envelopement, the cry of Amanda calling upon the name of Claude Montigny.

"Forward! faster, yet faster!" cried a voice in rage and apprehension; and with renewed application of whip and spur, the party tore along the road, shaking it as the prairie is shaken when it is swept over by a herd of buffaloes.

"Claude, Claude!" she again shrieked, and now in addition to the thick cowl, a huge hand was placed upon her mouth, a threat of instant death came from the terrible voice behind her, the grip tightened round her form, and, making her darkness yet darker, at that moment the clouds, that had been lately gathering, covered the moon. Soon the way divided before them. To the left it meandered half hidden with trees, to the right it loomed straight and open, leading to Montreal, and the motion of the horses, now abreast and flinging foam from their bits, seemed like the tossing of the boiling rapids, and amidst the thunder of the hoofs the hoarse voice of him who rode behind her, hissing with earnestness and fear like an excited Python, exclaimed:

F

"Brother, and you, master Imp, make for the city; away!" And soon, from the diminished sound, she knew that they had parted company with a portion of her convoy. She could hear, too, that the remaining horseman of the four, for that had been the number, had now fallen into the rear, and, soon, she thought she heard through her mufflings a voice crying as if commanding them to stay; and again she heard it, but it had grown fainter, and wider from the track they were pursuing, and now nothing was heard but the sound of their impetuous course through the wood. This was soon cleared, when their speed seemed to relax, and the hard breathing of the overstrained beasts, proclaimed how much the chase had told upon them; and at last the veil was slightly raised, a large, coarse visage peered under it, and the hoarse voice enquired mockingly : "How fares my bird? We will let a little light into its cage, if it will promise to sing no more. What says my hooded crow?" and a titanic and convulsive hug followed, causing her to shrink with pain, and revolt in disgust and horror; feelings which changed to mortal apprehension, when the same lascivious looking ruffian bade his now sole male companion ride on before. The latter made no answer, but dashed up alongside, and gazed into the face of Amanda as he passed, with an air of curiosity mingled with admiration and respect. There was in him a likeness to the sinistrous countenanced ogre behind her; yet he was a rather handsome young fellow; and as the wind, caused by their rapid course, blew backward his long, curly hair, he exhibited a cast of honesty and openness in his aspect. The other seemed to be impatient at his lingering, and growled :

"Don't hang glowering here; forwards, and warn me if any one approaches, that I may cover up this toy." And whilst the monster readjusted the cowl to the face of Amanda, his comrade again pricked the panting sides of his own horse, that being lightlier laden than its fellow, easily shot ahead. And thus they swept along the road, whilst the rising breeze still drove the clouds over the face of the moon, and the race seemed to have its fantastic counterpart in the wrack of the sky. And now they silently journeyed, avoiding village and hamlet, by making wide detours; but, in spite of their precautions, arousing the bark of many a solitary cur, as they swept by each homestead like an apparition. Even these incidents, and possible chances for her rescue at length ceased, and the despairing Amanda, too proud to vainly beg for her release from her stubborn captors, drew the hood again over her face, and in the double darkness called upon Heaven to be her protector and deliverer. That Claude had heard her cries she felt assured; that he had pursued a portion of her abductors towards Montreal, and would continue his efforts, with those of her guardian and the inmates of Stillyside, to find and recover her she did not doubt; but in the meantime what might she not have to endure? And shrinking from the contemplation of the uncertain gulf before her, she was at length recalled to a sense of external things, by a sudden change of sound, from that of the clatter of the horses' hoofs on the hard road, to one like the roll of a distant peal of thunder, and telling her they were crossing a rude wooden bridge, that led from the Island to the main. Then for the first time the riders permanently abated their speed, and their prisoner enquired of them whither they were carrying her.

"Never mind that, my pretty passenger pigeon," replied the elder with a ghoul-like grin; "you will not require to find your way back this year." And the foaming, exhausted animals, relieved from the trying gallop, dropped into a feeble trot or lazy canter, whilst Amanda gazed wistfully around to discover some glimpse of dawn. No certain sign of it, however, could she perceive on the circle of the horizon, though all around there showed the whitened eaves of the roof of gloomy clouds. Her companions, too, casting jealous glances at each other in the obscurity, had become more mutually taciturn; and the wind, that during the previous part of their flight had risen, as if to be in keeping with the current violence, had now fallen to a calm; and, proceeding thus, she continued to tell the terrors of her situation, as they alternately glided through the gloom of the clearing, or plunged into the denser darkness of the forest; till at last she was startled by something leaping against her feet, followed by the pleased but stifled barking of a huge hound close by her, and at the same instant she saw a woman bearing a lighted candle in her hand, emerge from a hovel on the road side. The next moment the party were halted before it, and the woman, holding up her light, shed its beams upon the face and form of Amanda, whose arrival she seemed to have been expecting; and after having fixed her eyes searchingly upon her, turned them with a familiar and significant look on the still seated ruffian. The light illuminated her own countenance as much as that of Amanda, who, repelled by her manners and appearance, sat motionless, and checked the appeal that was rising to her lips. The redoubtable rider dismounted awkwardly from behind her, half dragged her from the tall beast, and hurried her into the house. The woman followed, and having closed the door, placed the candle on a table, and sat down by the fire; when Amanda, still standing in the midst of the miserable room, began:

"Woman, what place is this? Where am I, and why have I been brought hither?" then bursting into passionate grief: "Oh, woman, woman, whosoever you are, save me, I implore you, from this man," and with the words she sprang towards the door; but the churlish giant, guessing her intention, intercepted, and bore her back, saying: "Keep quiet, gentle lady; have patience, bashful beauty; sit down, sit down; come pet, come." And he made as if to approach her; when, forgetting the hazard of her position, and inspired with returning native courage, with her heart swelling with womanly indignation, and looking the vast figure in the face, she cried with an utterance tremulous from grief and scorn: "Whither have you brought me, villain, and for what end? Sirrah, come no nearer me: I am polluted by your touch. Out, shameless wretch!" and again she rushed towards the door, but found it resist her utmost efforts: and, baffled, turning within, she once more addressed herself to the female, who was now carelessly warming herself before some embers on the hearth.

"Woman," she said, "for that you are one your form and garb assure me, though your behaviour gives your exterior the lie; woman, if you be one, save me. Charge this man—for you have influence with him—to liberate me; oh! charge him to release me. Turn me into the lane, into the field, or where you will; but let me leave this house without delay."

The female, with a grim smile, bade her recompose herself; whilst the burly brute doggedly hinted to her that she would have to remain some time in those parts, and might as well sit down and be content. Perplexed at this second announcement of her intended restriction, Amanda stood mute in fear and horror. To arouse the creature in whose power she was might be immediately dangerous, but, for a moment, to seem resigned to her abduction was impossible. Trembling with dismay and sickening with apprehension, her limbs would scarcely sustain her; and as she mentally revolved, looking wistfully around, as if to spy any nook or cranny for escape, she at last exclaimed:

"Again, I ask, why am I brought hither? Outlaw, who are you? wherein have I wronged you, that you should drag me to I know not where? What place is this, and why have you come with men as heartless as yourself, stealing me from my home to bring me hither, and cast me into this den?" and her bosom filled as she ended; but her hearer, knowing no compunction, only answered with a sneer: "To clip your wings, madam," then gave a low laugh, as if of self-applause at his quickness of repartee, or the prospect of her humiliation, and added: "Pray, miss, retire; you have not been abed to-night, and watching is not good for English ladies' eyes."

"Shameless!" she cried, looking upon him with unmitigable disdain, "how dare you hint at rest

within these walls? Return me to the spot whence
you have taken me; render me to my home, so
desecrated, so invaded by such felonious feet as yours.
Felon, convey me to my home at Stillyside, and there
reinstate me; if indeed you have the heart, as you
have the outward semblance, of a man;" and, in spite
of her resentment, she burst into a flood of tears.

But not even woman's tears could move his stolid
disposition, or melt his stony heart; and, looking at her
with an expression akin to contempt, he demanded :

"What, take the bird back to the bush where we
have caught it? No. Besides at present you have
taken a long-enough ride, and when next you journey
it must be further in the same direction. You shall
see the world, and learn how wide it is; you shall
have most excellent French society."

"Oh, keep me, heaven, from such society as yours,"
she ejaculated :—"base man!—but do you know to
what you have exposed yourself? Beware; I am
not without friends both subtle and strong, and one
of whom will not be slow to punish you for this outrage. Release me, stranger, or you shall be visited
with his vengeance, not to be trifled with, not to be
risked with safety."

"Ah, the old advocate," exclaimed the giant, with
more bitterness than he had hitherto manifested;
"Outrage! he has himself outraged too many of our
race."

"Ay, that he has;" the woman chimed in, whilst
her eyes suddenly glared dilating, and she looked
menacingly at Amanda; "there is Robitaille, and
Lamoureux, and Paille, and myself, and Babet Blais,—
poor Babet! but her boy, *his* boy, his own son, has

paid him down with sorrow, *he* has punished him ;—
ha! ha!" and both she and her Gorgon-like guest
laughed a meaning and triumphant laugh, whilst
Amanda yet stood there to be baited by the brutish
man and the lost, revengeful woman, the latter of
whom thus continued to vent her spleen : " Mistress,
what are you but an English interloper ? Girl, how
can we endure you ? Do you not despise us ? Do you
not insult, despoil, dishonor us ? Do you not covet
our lands, do you not reap the taxes, take the trade ?
Would you not all be Seigneurs ? What shall we
give you that you have not already taken ! Ah, out
upon you, my young mistress ! Think it well if you
should not receive what I shall not now name to
you,—your guardian's gift to many a maiden—and
worse ;" she added between her teeth ; " death,
death," and turned away scowling.

"Return me to my home, or worse than death
awaits you;" cried Amanda; "endless infamy; hated
of our race, despised of your's, disowned by both."

But the woman by this time had begun to busy
herself in piling new logs upon the fire, and the colos-
sus, her companion, after having scanned the apartment, seemingly to ascertain whether it was to be
trusted to retain the prisoner, at length, satisfied
with the result of his scrutiny, unlocked the door
with the key which he drew from his pocket, and
bestowing a bow of mock respect upon Amanda, who
affected not to perceive it, departed ; and she, without
vouchsafing a look upon her feminine but callous
jailor, sank upon a chair in silence.

CHAPTER XII.

" Ring the alarm bell.'
Macbeth.

The abductors of Amanda were no other than the
three sons of Andre Duchatel, along with the vindictive Narcisse acting as their guide.   He and
Alphonse Duchatel, at the branching of the road, had
parted company with the others, and so drawn upon
themselves the pursuer, Claude Montigny, who being
magnificently mounted gained fast upon them, till
fearing to be overtaken they leaped from their horses,
and taking to their heels concealed themselves amongst
the trees that covered the side of the mountain, and
where no rider could follow.   Claude then saw that he
had been the dupe of a stratagem ; and after galloping
across the country, struck the road that he had been
decoyed from following ; then urging his horse in the
direction which he supposed the principal abductors
had pursued, he at length in despair left it, and again
clearing fence and brook, held his course towards the
city of Montreal, where he arrived betwixt midnight
and dawn, and with the butt of his riding-whip
knocked at the advocate's door.

The old man was dreaming of the apparently fair
fortune of Amanda ; of the ingenuous Claude, and of
his father, the importunate and imperious Seigneur,
when the clang rung through the mansion, and rudely
dispelled his visions.   At first he was doubtful as to

the reality of the alarm, and was dropping again to sleep, when once more the riding-whip sent the startling summons, and leaping from his bed, he threw open the window, and putting his head out, gruffly demanded, who was there.

"Claude Montigny," was answered from beneath.

"And what wants Claude Montigny at this hour?" asked the advocate, who now perceived the figures of steed and dismounted rider beneath him in the obscurity.

"Dress instantly, and quick come down," was the reply. The window closed, and in a few minutes the advocate, with his morning gown thrown over him, opened the door.

"Why how is this?" he demanded in astonishment, as he beheld Claude on the footwalk, whip in one hand, and with the other holding his horse by the bridle.

Claude stood silent.

"How is this?" reiterated the advocate: "Out with it, man. Is your father wild? does he threaten to disinherit you?"

"Not that, but worse:" Claude answered; "worse than your worst suspicions, and it may be worse than the death of one you much regard."

"Has any thing evil happened to my ward?" asked the advocate, exhibiting alarm. "Why do you pause? Inform me quickly."

"Too quickly, perhaps, I shall inform you," replied Claude, deprecatingly. "Something evil has happened to your ward. Arm yourself now with firmness, and be calm; be cool in judgment, prompt in execution; you who can counsel others, now prepare to be the best counsellor to yourself."

"What act shall follow this preamble?" said the lawyer, raising his thick, white, shaggy eyebrows in enquiring wonder: "Go on, go on;" he commanded in a short, gasping utterance; "declare the pains and penalties. She lives? Amanda lives? Has she proved false? You have not lost her?"

"Lost her! oh!" exclaimed Claude, unable to curb his emotion.

"Nay, confess it; announce the worst; the broadest misfortune; my ears are open for it," pursued the other.

"But I have no heart, no tongue to fill them with my dire news," Claude stammered, and the advocate resumed, growing impatient:

"Of my ward what can you tell me that is untoward? Of myself say anything: foretell disaster, prophecy my death;—but what of her?—you say she lives?"

"She does."

"Is well?"

Claude shook his head, and remained silent.

"Sir, let your lips pronounce my doom at once," said the advocate, striving to be calm, yet alarmed and irritated; "Proceed:—I am ashamed to say it, but I tremble. What has befallen my ward, what trouble has alighted on my child?—for so I call her. Claude Montigny, what is it brings you here betwixt night and day, with tidings that you falter to deliver?"

"Calm yourself;" counselled Claude in a warning tone.

"I will;" answered the advocate; "I do;—resolve me quickly."

"I fear to do so," Montigny uttered pathetically, as if his resolution had suddenly given way.

" Let me hear it, torture me no longer :" cried the
advocate imperatively : " Perfect knowledge, perhaps,
may stun me; but far worse to bear than were a shower
of vitriol poured on a green wound, are these distilled,
dire drops of apprehension.   Sir, are you guilty that
you thus stand dumb ?   What have you done injurious towards my ward, that you so linger upon the
street, and to my queries but gaze like one demented ?
Sir, I charge you, tell me without more reserve or
hesitation, lest at last I listen to you with less of fear
than of anger.   You have been——"

" The innocent accessory, I fear, to others' villany,"
Claude interrupted; " still, hear me," he continued,
" and forgive me if I bring you tidings that shall
hang as heavy on your soul as lead; yet have given
me the leaden bullet's swiftness, or that of the
blast, to waft them hither, blasting, to yourself.—
Sir, you have been robbed, bereaved; the star of
Stillyside is set,—or, worse, plucked from its firma-
ment; my life, my lady, oh, my new-made love, your
peerless ward is stolen."

" Stolen !" the advocate echoed.

" Stolen; even from my very arms is plucked,"
continued Claude.

" Ill-freighted messenger," groaned the old lawyer;
" stolen! oh, Montigny, you have stolen half the
strength from these old limbs, and strained the
sinews that have never bent before, neither to man
nor to misfortune.   Stolen! How stolen? It is false;
you jest, you mean that you yourself have stolen
her,—have stolen her heart; you know I lately
caught you in the act;—but, for her person, she
would not, could not, give it you without my leave.

Montigny, you have not stolen together to the church?—but this is in the street; come in."

Claude tied his courser to a young maple that grew near the door; and, whilst he was doing so, the advocate retired within, murmuring: "Montigny, Seigneur Montigny, this is your work, and yet may prove the dearest piece of petty larceny that ever man committed; as dear as would have been to have furnished the dower you refused me. No;" he continued musing, "trouble does not spring from out of the ground. Then whence comes this? Who hates me?" he continued sharply; "Covets her? Whom would her absence serve? who, except the father of yon boy, the Sieur Montigny?" and he had scarcely finished his soliloquy when he was rejoined by Claude, who, straightway in the obscurity of the library, related to him the adventure of the night.

The old man listened in silence, but his bosom heaved, and when Claude had ceased, he grasped him by the hand and exclaimed:

"Montigny, we are bound together in that girl, the outrage upon whom has made us rivals in the task to find and rescue her. Yet are you sure the voice you heard was her's? You did not see her carried off; you only heard, or thought you heard, her cry. You may have been deceived. Hasten back to Stillyside. She may be there now sleeping between the unruffled sheets, making them sweeter than the perfuming lavender;—if she be not—why then—alas! what then?" And he struck his palm against his brow, holding it there, perplexed, revolving.

"You say you heard your name pronounced?" he enquired at length.

"I did," said Claude, unhesitatingly; and this seemed to satisfy the lawyer's doubts, and, rising, he said, shaking his companion by the hand: "Montigny, go. Beat up the bush at Stillyside; and if she be not there,—why all the country side shall be roused to find and bring her back. But, Claude, she is safe. Yet hie you thither; mount again your horse, and bring me word before the day breaks: begone." And in a few moments Claude was scouring back to Stillyside, and the advocate ruminating alone amidst the shadows of his library.

CHAPTER XIII.

"This noble gentleman, Lord Titus here,
Is in opinion, and in honor, wronged;
That in the rescue of Lavinia,
With his own hand did slay his youngest son "

Titus Andronicus.

The elder Montigny, wrathful and irresolute, and like a beast in the toils, had yesterday again visited the advocate on the same errand as before, and with a like unsatisfactory result.   But instead of returning to Mainville he had proceeded to the Duchatel Manor House; partly for counsel, but chiefly to ascertain whether its owner—who, he deemed, had an equal interest with himself in the removal of Amanda —would join with him in furnishing the demanded dower.   The subject was broached privately to the shrewd and worldly André, who on hearing it propounded swore indignantly at the advocate's audacity, and roundly refused to accede to any such appropriation of his substance: so after fierce denunciations of the insolence of upstart English adventurers, and censure of the infatuation of young fellows in affairs of the heart, the theme was dropped for the present, and the remainder of the day spent in looking over the estate, and in those attentions that are usually bestowed on a visitor, be he ever so familiar a one, much more when he is both distinguished and in prospective relationship.   The next day the topic was resumed, but this time in the presence of Samson

Duchatel, as he sat yawning between asleep and awake, but who, on hearing the conversation, aroused himself, and bade Montigny be easy, and not dream of endowing the foreigner, since he, Samson, had already secured the troublesome fair one. Montigny took little notice of this, thinking it to be but the jest or boast, or, at furthest, merely the loose announcement of the intention of the unscrupulous giant; who soon afterwards invited him to walk abroad. The company of Samson was not coveted by the more refined and anxious Seigneur, but the former pressed him, and he thought that locomotion might divert his mind from the contemplation of the coming degradation and folly of his son. He consented, and issuing from the ancient and flower-festooned porch of the Manor House, they walked along in mid-morning of late September, the drowsy charms of the summer's faded foliage just awakening to a resurrection in the glorified beauty of Autumn; and, almost in silence, they proceeded along the road or lane, till they came to the dubious dwelling where, some hours before, Amanda was left a prisoner. The sullen and sloven-looking female who had received her was now dressed in gaudy attire, and saluted them as they entered, at the same time casting a look of enquiry and surprise into the face of Samson, and of suspicion on the Seigneur.

"Bring up the body of your prisoner;" growled the former, loudly, as he threw his huge frame into an arm-chair. "Come, habeas corpus, habeas corpus. Now, if we had Alphonse here," he continued, "he could repeat the whole writ in Latin. Habeas corpus, habeas corpus," muttered the puzzled savage,

fumbling in his brains for the context, "habeas corpus, habeas corpus;—" then, relinquishing the vain
search, and addressing himself to the woman, at the
same time elevating his voice, he vociferated: "Hillo,
come, lady sheriff, bring up the body of your prisoner,
I say;" when, as if in obedience to the call of a
magician, a door opened, and from an inner room,
with face flushed, brow dark and fretted with indignation, lips pouting, breast heaving, and her eyes
overflowing with tears, in bounded his sister, Seraphine Duchatel, exclaiming: "And is this the creature that has stood between me and Claude? and
brought here, too, to flout me to my face! I'll not
endure it;" and she burst into a fresh torrent of
tears.

"Who has stood between you, girl?" enquired the
brother, half teasingly, half tenderly: "if there be
a stump between here and Mainville that hinders
you from driving your carriage thither, tell me, and
we'll pull it up as quickly as Doctor Lanctot would
pull you a tooth out."

"You have done well, indeed," continued the angry
girl, weeping, and not minding his clumsy badinage,
"you have done well indeed, to bring her here to
answer me, to scorn me, to defy me, to parade herself
before me, to stand in my presence as proud as any
peacock,—only not half so beautiful."

"Fine feathers make fine birds, Phin," drily
retorted her brother.

"She is not fine, and if she be, she shall be plucked
of her finery;" exclaimed the sister: "I'll tear her
eyes out; what business has she to look at *me*, and
speak so insolently? I'll have her face flayed; her

F

hair shall be plucked up by the roots;" and she stamped with her little foot.

"We'll have her scalped, girl!" condoled her brother.

"Yes, this is the way you always think to manage me; by laughing at me," cried the spoiled child, in renewed agony of tears.

"Why, what is the matter?" demanded the Seigneur, wondering, and startled by these threatening allusions: "What is the meaning of all this, Samson?"

"Oll," answered the latter, striving to perpetrate a pun, "Only that we have brought Phin a hand-maiden, and she finds her *hand*somer than is agreeable;—but there is many a servant comelier than the mistress."

"Let me behold this Paragon," said the Seigneur, at the same time rising, and moving towards the door of the inner room, that had been left ajar by the rude Seraphine, in her indignant exit. Pushing it slowly open, he beheld Amanda, with half-averted form, seated upon a chair, her head bowed, but her face wearing an expression of proud serenity mixed with grief. His first impulse was to retire; but pity, respect, admiration, and even awe, bound him to the spot, and he remained gazing till curiosity and commiseration alike combined to induce him to address a figure so incongruous with that mean place, and whose majestic sorrow seemed too sacred for interruption.

"Young lady, by your leave; pray pardon me; but can a stranger be of service to you?" he at length enquired.

Amanda looked upward. "Oh, if you are, as you

seem to be, a gentleman, do not leave me;" she exclaimed beseechingly, as she slowly rose and approached him: "do not leave me, but convey me back to Stillyside, from whence I have been stolen by that man. Oh, sir, you do not know with what a load of thanks its owner will repay you, should you rescue me from this base durance."

The seigneur looked enquiringly at Samson, but the latter seemed more disposed to wait to see how the seigneur regarded the appeal, than to reply to the tacit question.

"Why have you been brought hither, and against your will?" resumed the seigneur, respectfully.

"I am as yet ignorant of the cause;" she answered: "I do not know, I cannot divine, why I am here a prisoner."

"She does know;" fiercely interrupted the sobbing Seraphine, "She does, she does," she reiterated, and seemed disposed to fly at her tooth and nail. "She knows she is a bold and wicked creature,—she, she, she; she is a, a,—I dont know what she is;" she cried, spurting out the last words in a paroxysm of sorrow and vexation, and flung herself into a chair sobbing hysterically, with toilet and temper alike disordered.

"Calm yourself, Seraphine," said the Seigneur.

"Yes, calm thyself, girl." echoed the ponderous Samson. "Why, what a wild duck thou art, sister, flapping and quacking because an unshotted barrel has been fired at thee. She is an unshotted gun, she has no name; and what is a thing without a name? nothing: for if it were something it would have been called something. What thing is there—that is a

thing—that has not got what a pudding has? a name,"
and he laughed till his sides shook, and drawing a
pouch from his pocket, took thence a quid of tobacco,
and put it into his cheek, at the same time playfully
offering another to the outraged Seraphine, who petu-
lently dashed it from his fingers, and affected to bridle
at the insult.

Meantime Amanda stood in silent sadness, and the
Seigneur, who had been watching her during the
heartless flirtation between the brother and sister,
advanced one pace into the room, and said : " I know
your story, and have reason to be angry, not so much
with you as with my son, whom, I believe, you are
acquainted with, one Claude Montigny."   Amanda
turned away her face and blushed.

" You do know him I perceive," the Seigneur continued, " and if by chance he has happened to know
you I do not blame him, much less can I blame yourself: but, lady, remember," and the proud Montigny
advanced, and bending over her whilst his voice fell,
as if it were intended for her ear alone, said " remember, we are not all of the same degree, though Heaven
has fashioned all of the same clay.   The proudest and
the wealthiest in Canada might hail you as a daughter ;
but old prescription, antecedents, prospects, all com-
bine to render impossible your union with my son."

Amanda blushed yet deeper, and both of them
stood for awhile embarrassed, but at length she said
falteringly, and glowing like a crimson poppy in her
confusion :

" I own it just that you should urge these large
considerations ; yet, believe me, sir, I have been pas-
sive in this matter, and have not sought your son's

" Meantime Amanda stood in silent sadness, and the Seigneur advanced one pace into the room."

acquaintance; neither, indeed, has he, if he be rightly judged, (and you would not wrong your son), perhaps, sought mine; for it would seem there are amities that Providence provides for us, without our will or knowledge. It was accident that brought us face to face; as we observe the sun and moon—that are separate in their seasons, and withal so different in their glory's given degree—brought monthly, and as if fortuitously, though, in reality, by eternal, fixed design, into conjunctive presence amidst the sky.

Yet who shall blame the sun and moon for that?

"None," said the Seigneur.

"Then let no one blame your son and me," continued Amanda, "if Heaven, perhaps to try us, has ordained that our paths should cross each other, as might two strange and diverse celestial bodies pass apparently too hazardously near each other in their appointed orbits. For the rest, forgive me, sir, and may He who best knows what is for the benefit of his creatures, and who sometimes for their good, sees it right that they should suffer wrongfully, assist me. Since this has pleased Him, I bow, and bear it the best I may, and trust too, that He will, in His good pleasure, deliver me from this that He has permitted to fall upon me, my present sad and dangerous estate of a poor prisoner here."

"Heaven will indeed rescue you from this infamous restraint, and I will gladly be its minister," returned the Seigneur, melted almost to love with pity, and dropping a tear; "none shall detain you here; you are safe. Let me, myself—if thereby to some extent may be atoned to you the wrong you have sustained in being hurried hither—conduct you to your guardian."

"And raise the devil !—ay, and bring him here : her guardian is his half brother," suddenly roared Samson in surprise and terror. "No, Montigny, she has given too much trouble in the catching to be so lightly released. Besides, is she to be still allowed to stand between her betters. Leave her with me."

"Yes, leave her with Samson," cried the sulking Seraphine, starting up in her chair. "He has known better girls, and handsomer, too;—umph! how much men can be mistaken. It is wonderful that Claude should covet her. Take her to her guardian! fie, Monsieur Montigny," and half turning away in her seat with scorn and disgust, she cast a look of ineffable hatred and disdain at the suppliant Amanda, whilst the woman of the house fixed her jealousy-filled eyes on Samson as he murmured : "She shall not go : she is my prisoner."

"She must return with me, sir, said the Seigneur, quietly but firmly. "Are you not aware how great is the penalty that you have incurred by this disgraceful scandal? Think it fortunate if you shall be able in any way to compound for it with the lady's guardian. Seraphine, mollify your indignation towards one who has not meant to thwart you. Return to the hall with your brother, whilst I conduct this injured lady to the parsonage, to remain there until I can escort her home, and (as I hope) with the aid of her intercession, obtain the pardon of her cruel abductors."

"It is you that is cruel:" cried the weeping Seraphine: "it is Claude that is cruel. Not meant to thwart me! she *has* thwarted me, and you encourage her, you justify her, Monsieur Montigny."

"We will crucify her," cried Samson.

"Say no more," commanded the seigneur: "you are both of you ignorant of the heinous nature of what you have done. Her guardian has the power to punish you. Tremble lest he should exercise it." And, with these words, he gave his arm to Amanda, and, passing amidst the scowling trio, led her from the place.

CHAPTER XIV.

"Confess the truth."
Measure for Measure.

"You would pluck out the heart of my mystery."
Hamlet.

Claude Montigny rode to Stillyside and back, and was again with the advocate within the hour. To conceive the terror and outcry in that quiet dwelling, when its inmates ascertained that Amanda was missing, let the reader recall the commotion in the castle of Macbeth, when on the morning following his fatal entrance beneath its battlements, it is discovered that the royal Duncan has been murdered. As vehement and as wild as when the distracted Macduff, in frantic tones and with wringing hands, declares to the assembling sons and thanes of the ill-starred monarch, that, "confusion now has made its masterpiece, most sacrilegeous murder has broken open the Lord's anointed temple, and stolen hence the life o' the building," was the outcry and disorder on the discovery of Amanda's absence; and the wail and lamentation rung in Claude's ear as he rode away from the gate to return to Montreal, where, still pacing the library, the advocate anxiously awaited him. By the ratiocination, as well as by the intuition, of the old man, the seigneur of Mainville was reasonably to be suspected of being at least an accessory to the stealing of Amanda. Claude, too, was not unvisited by suspicions of his father's complicity;

but thrust the dishonoring doubts from him, as might a suffering saint dismiss hard thoughts of the dealings of Providence towards himself. Each thought more than he expressed to the other, but at length the advocate communicated to Claude his injurious suspicions, acquainting him with the fact and nature of his father's visits to his office; when Claude, in turn, informed the advocate of the long cherished project of an alliance between the houses of Duchatel and Montigny. This information not only confirmed, but widened the field of the advocate's fears. He was aware also of the lawless character of Duchatel's sons; and recollected to have heard that the youngest was a comrade of Narcisse, who, he likewise knew, entertained a covert spite against Amanda, and, for his mother's sake, a rankling dislike of Mona Macdonald. Against both of these his umbrage might be supposed to have been heated by his recent ignominious expulsion from Stillyside; and to gratify this resentment he might now be executing some scheme of revenge, wherein, from his intimacy with the young Duchatel, he could know that that family had cause to be ready to assist him. Here was a clue to the recovery of his ward:—in legal parlance, here was a prima facie case; and it but remained to find and prosecute the criminals. To seize his son, and, by threats or promises, extract a confession from him was the first idea. But where was the errant and suspected Narcisse to be found? His father knew he was absent, so the mother was summoned. She came, but advanced no further than the threshold of the room, and fell a trembling with fear, behaviour that she would fain have dissembled to be from cold,

for, with the divination with which guilt endows its
subject, she at once knew that the stranger was the
young Montigny, and herself had been cited in order
to suffer a searching cross-examination.

"Woman," said the advocate sternly, and wheeling
his arm-chair round so as to face her, "Woman, where
is your son?"

"Helas!" she exclaimed, and shrugged her shoulders,
as much as to say, "I don't know where he is;" and
smiled a rueful smile.

"No grinning now," cried the lawyer, raising his
finger and shaking it at her, and frowning as he was
wont to do when he wished to intimidate a witness,
"no grinning now, madam. Will you pretend to say
you know nothing of where he was last night, where
he is at present?

"Helas!" again exclaimed the affrighted Babet:
"sir you forget yourself. Last night? Why it is
yet night. Open the shutters and put out the lamp,
and you will still be in darkness. Let me return to
bed."

"Babet Blais, many a better woman than you have
I wished bedridden," the advocate cried with bitterness. "Beshrew me, but your answer. Remember I
am flint if you are steel, hence the less often we are
smitten together in this enquiry, the fewer may be
the revealing sparks. Babet Blais, here is an affair
of blackest tinder, whereon your bated breath has
blown already, until it glows upon your guilty face,
as grimly as the lurid East that brews a rainy day,
to you the type of tears."

"What do you mean?" demanded the half mysti-
fied and still dissembling woman, in terror.

"Babet Blais, here is an affair of blackest tinder whereon your bated breath has blown already, until it glows upon your guilty face."

"What do I mean? I mean that you shall tell me where your son was during the last night, and where he is now."

"Where he is *now?*" echoed Babet, "Last night? it is now night, or only just near dawning."

"Yes, we are near the dawning," mocked the old man, with loud, relentless equivoque. "Madam, shed here the sunbeams of your highest intelligence; clear the dull atmosphere of your soul from fog; and let us see and hear respecting this occurrence, all that yourself have seen, and heard, and known."

"Master, I know nothing," said she, "what affair?" enquired the woman, fitfully.

"Is Narcisse at home?" bellowed the advocate, quivering with excitement, and red to the roots of his white hair with wrath. "Evil betide me that he should have ever made here his home;" he continued. "Who called him hither? I? No, no; I called for aught that might see fit to come, conditioned that it came in human guise; but yonder frothy fool, yon swarthy pigmy, I did not summon him. I called for anything of earth, but Heaven (to punish me) straight passed the unhallowed call to hell, that sent me up a demon." The apartment resounded with the last word, and still the old man's voice was heard like the departing rumble of a thunder peal, as he continued, with clasped hands and upturned eyes, whilst his countenance assumed an air of singular elevation, passionately exclaiming: "Oh, that a man who could have entertained the gods with high conceits and philosophic parle,—could have communed with spirits of the skies, should be assailed and pestered from the pit!—Go on, woman, we will exorcise you, we

will purge you, though you be fouler than the Augean
stable, that had been left uncleaned for thirty years;
ay, though you be as foul as is the stall that holds the
grimy company of the lost, and which goes uncleaned
for ever. Proceed, I charge thee!" and the fierce-
eyed lawyer sat dilated and erect in his chair, glaring
upon her like a serpent rearing its crest from amidst
its coils, as he waited for an answer.

"I cannot, I know no further," she said at length,
with meek doggedness.

"What say you?" exclaimed the advocate, almost
screaming with astonishment.

"I know no further; I know nothing," she replied.

"Assist me, patience, to confound this creature!
Nothing! you know all;" he shouted. "All, I say,
all; for never had such a mother such a son, but he
did pour out all his purposes, all the infernal cornu-
copia, into her breast from his. You have no secrets
between you; you, his mother, know all his course;
his thoughts, intents, conspiracies and plots; his
loves, his hates, his loose, irregular life; his merry
moments, and his moods of malice. I charge thee,
tell us where he was last night, where yesterday,
where he is now, and where he will be to-morrow."

"Monsieur, I know no more, know nothing," cried
the woman, appealing to Claude. "My master is
mad," and, bursting into tears, began: "Here have
I been his housekeeper twenty years—"

"Twenty years too long," vociferated the advocate.
"One half the period that heaven was vexed with a
stiff-necked generation have I endured you, Babet.
Housekeeper! eh? Keeper of the King's conscience
next, a she Lord Chancellor,—but continue: call

yourself Keeper of the Seals, and mistress—or master either—of the Rolls, so you unroll your secret. Tell all you may; empty your flask of falsehood, then at the bottom we may find some sediment of truth. Commence; don't count upon concealment. I will wring the truth from you, though it shall ooze out drop by drop, and each drop be a portion of your life."

Babet was still silent, but the lawyer pursued:

"Oh, toad, ugly and venomous, you have a precious jewel in your head; deliver it; discover to myself and to this gentleman all that you know about your son's late conduct. Speak, or you shall have your closed lips forced apart, or there shall be found and set you such tormenting penance, that you shall sue with speed to make confession. What! still silent? Bathe no longer that face with tears. Out on thee, crocodile! Oh, that those trite tears were scales, falling, to leave you bare and vulnerable to arrows of adjurement; then, with patience I could see them fall as fast as flakes of snow in winter, till thou wert as white as Judge's ermine with them! Creature, hast thou nothing plausible, nothing for us, nothing for him, nor me?"

"Nothing for you, nor for this gentleman," she answered quietly.

"Do not imagine him to be so gentle, neither. Though he dwells staid and silent, he is a roaring lion, that should I let slip may soon devour thee, Babet. Overweening woman, you do not know how much you and yours have wronged him," said the advocate.

Claude had heard all this without speaking, but now he interposed, to try persuasion.

"Good Babet," said he, soothingly, "if you are aware of anything untoward of Monsieur's ward, and will declare it, I guarantee to you, not only a condonation for your son, if he have in any shape conspired against her, but a reward so weighty for yourself, that you shall bless the hour that you were awoke so early to be scolded. What do you know of the lost lady of Stillyside?"

At these words a smile covered her face, as if of satisfaction at good news; then, shrugging her shoulders, she languidly asked: "Is she missing?" and added, "Helas! then others have an absent child, as well as I," and shook her head; and, with another shrug, continued, as if subsiding into herself, and in a tone of combined decision and sadness: "I know nothing of the lady, nothing of my boy. Heaven grant my son is safe, my poor Narcisse, and that he may not return and meet his cruel father, who so hates him;" and she brushed away a tear from her cheek.

"Heaven grant indeed we do not meet at present!" ejaculated the foiled advocate; "for if we did, I might so far exceed a parent's punitory privilege, that I should win but blame from the blind world instead of sympathy. Begone, vampire," and she vanished like a ghost at cockcrow.

That smile of her's at the mention of Amanda missing, had been caught by the advocate's keen eye, and convinced him that she and her son were accessories to the felony of the night. Brief consultation now sufficed between him and Claude, who also felt convinced of her complicity. Light began to glimmer amidst the darkness of the situation, and, as it kindled into a dreary dawn, as might a new scene amongst dissolving views, shadowy and sinistrous amidst it seemed to loom the figures of the Duchatels; and, before the sun had risen, Claude, winged equally with hope and indignation, was posting towards Montbœuf. The advocate threw himself upon a couch, and he would fain have thrown up his brief of that day, but it was for a case involving capital punishment, and, at the eleventh hour, to have deserted his client would have brought upon himself, not only professional dishonor, but guilt. Hence, with heavy heart and unwilling faculties he bent his attention to the study of the important case, whilst at intervals he swallowed a portion of the morning's meal, that at the usual hour was silently placed before him; and at last, with an inexpressible sadness and boding, he left the stillness of his home for the walls of the busy and exciting arena of the criminal court.

CHAPTER XV.

"Oh, what a rash and bloody deed is this !"
Hamlet.

"Shall blow the horrid deed in every eye."
Macbeth.

The Court had been opened, and was crowded with lawyers, petit jurors, witnesses, and excited spectators. A criminal trial of such interest as the present one had not occurred there for years ; and the business in the Civil Courts had virtually been adjourned, so great was the determination of the pleaders therein to be present, and witness the conducting of a case so calculated to call forth the powers of the renowned and venerable advocate. All conspired to show that an extraordinary scene was to be enacted there that day. The Judge was more than usually grave, attentive and deliberate; the Crown Prosecutor wary, and complete in his preparations ; the legal, technical, and clerical grounds of exception and demur, before the Crown was allowed to take up the burden of proof, were entered and explored by the advocate, as one who reconnoitres before committing his feet to dark and dangerous precincts, where any one of his advancing steps may prove to be fatal.

And now the case had been laid before the jury, and the witnesses for the prosecution, each as he testified touching the fearful crime laid to the charge of the prisoner at the bar, were being subjected to the terrible ordeal of a cross-examination by the advocate ;

who all eye all ear appeared, as in his earlier days;
quick to detect, prompt to demand, stern to insist, at
watch and ward at every point; so that his client
seemed to have found in him an irresistible champion,
and the crowd, to all of whom he was familiar, considered his success as certain, just as the veteran
soldiery anticipate a triumph from the General, who
has so often led them to victory that they deem him to
have become invincible. But to the thoughtful and
more observant, at times he showed signs of preoccu-
pation, strangely at variance with his present un-
doubted supremely master mood; and as the trial
proceeded these fits of wandering from the point
increased in duration and intensity. An anxious
expression settled on his countenance; his usually
energetic but measured movements when he was thus
engaged became irregular and nervous; and he frequently cast glances towards the entrance, as if
expecting the arrival of some one; and twice in the
midst of withering cross-examinations, stopped short
at the sight of individuals elbowing their way
through the crowd; gazing upon them enquiringly
and with an air of expectation, until, passing, they
became embedded in the serried mass of spectators;
when, with a look of disappointment, he resumed his
task, and again with consummate talent and charac-
teristic vigor, did battle for his client, whose dark
distinction in the dock went nigh unnoticed, from
the settled attention bestowed on his defender, just
as the prominently exhibited prize is sometimes
overlooked and temporarily forgotten, in the obser-
vation compelled to the rare skill shown by the com-
peting players.

G

But whilst the father was thus tasking every power
of his trained intellect, and crowning his career with
forensic fires, that now, in the evening of his genius,
burned even more signally, than they had done in
the midst of its meridian splendors ;—whilst thus
calling upon his great gifts, that, like to antique
jewels brightened by abrasion in the wearing, shone
yet the more from the polish of experience; and
while lending a legal learning that, as a rapier
which, ever ready and ever in requisition, has
acquired no rust, was the more available from long
practice combined with intuitive tact;—whilst all this
was passing in high and public court, the ignoble son
was awaking in a low lodging ; weary and stiff after
the raid of the past night, anxious and timid from a
sense of guilt, and fearful of a future calling to account.
His first wish was to discover whether his sire was
yet informed of the disappearance of his ward. He
knew that his father was retained in the trial
which had been fixed for that day, and had there
been any whom he could conveniently have sent to
ascertain whether or not the advocate was in court,
he would have despatched one thither, but he could
prevail upon none about him to go for love, and
money he had none to offer. His mother, alarmed
at her master's discovery of the participation by
Narcisse in their successful conspiracy, and not knowing where to find the latter, had despatched a messenger to the lodging of their bold and insolent accom-
plice, Alphonse Duchatel, requesting him to warn her
son to avoid his father during that day. But the
messenger failed to find him, and Narcisse at last
arose, dressed, and, prompted by a curiosity that

overcame his apprehensions, approached the Court House.

Meantime the advocate, tortured by increasing alarm, and with his imagination filling with tragic touches the picture of the possible fate of Amanda, had lost both recollection and temper; and for the first time when conducting a cross-examination, had been not merely baffled, but successfully bearded and insulted by an irritated witness, to relieve himself from whom, he was obliged abruptly to bid him leave the box. The occurrence stung him to the quick, though he strove to hide his chagrin;—no wonder. Taken at disadvantage, and in a moment of weakness, the old pleader was obliged to perceive that the wager of mental duel between himself and the witness had been decided against him; and to feel that, in an unsought encounter and fair affray, he had been publicly worsted. To add to his mortification, the witness walked from the box with the air of a conqueror, and cast an insolent look of triumph around the court and upon his antagonist, whose discomfiture was so signal as to be evident to judge, jurors, witnesses, spectators, all. Still more to increase the advocate's perturbation, the heat of the court had become excessive, and the rebuff— which, at an earlier period of his career, and with an unwounded heart, would have provoked only such a grim and threatening smile as a powerful wrestler might wear, when, in the careless security of proud contempt, he had been thrown by a boy— now, in the self-esteem of age and the anguish of bereavement, moved him almost to madness. Seizing his gown, he half cast it from his form, regardless of

decorum, and stood the picture of misery, rage, and
scorn.

Just then the court arose for a brief recess. Glad
to breathe for a moment the fresher air, the spectators retired, the jury returned into their room, the
sheriff and the crown prosecutor sauntered to their
respective offices, the panel of petit jurors escaped in
a body, the prisoner withdrew from the front of the
dock, and sat unseen, pondering his chances between
the gallows and an acquittal;—even the criers of the
court abandoned their posts, and the younger mem-
bers of the bar, who usually gathered round the
advocate on these occasions, greeting him with
pleasant compliments, and polite and reverent attentions, seeing him thus moody, drifted to the lobby,
and in it paid court to some other, and secondary
legal luminary who was there holding his levee.
For awhile the advocate was left alone; then, emerging through the large folding doors into the corridor
or lobby, now cumbered with the gossipping groups,
through which he passed, solitary and in his gown,
like Cæsar in his robe passing through the midst of
the conspirators, he proceeded past the doors of the
offices occupied by the various crown officials. None
spoke to the old man, he spoke to none, but his breast
burned in agony, and a cloud was on his brow, like
the smoke that wreathes around the crater of a vol-
cano. His eyes seemed to shoot forth sparks, and his
lips were muttering. Anger and sorrow were upon
his face, but, turning a corner in the building, he
was now hidden from the view of the multitude, and
strode along the main corridor towards the huge
double staircase that, midway therein, wound down

"Demon ! degenerate dog ! where hast thou been walking to and fro on the earth ?"

to the dim entrance hall, that was divided by ponderous doors from the esplanade between the building and the busy street. A low, massive balustrade guarded the bridge-like portion of the corridor that hung between the heads of the twin flights of stairs, and whence, on looking down, was seen the paved abyss below. Approaching this part, what did he behold but the truant Narcisse, unconscious of his presence, ascending one of these flights of stairs. At the sight of him the gloomy elements of his soul seemed to flash within him and explode, rending all resolution of restraint, and leaving him a puppet of some destructive power, as he stood eyeing his son's approach, as the cat eyes that of the marauding mouse, motionless, allowing the culprit to draw near, until, detected, he stood, too nigh to retreat, too terrified to advance, and, as the fascinated bird drops into the open jaws of the serpent, fell resistless into the grasp of the advocate's extended hand. Then, as the firedamp when met by the miner's candle must explode, or as the liberated lightning must rend the cloud, though the latter be near Jove's throne, so the frenzied father, regardless, nay, forgetful, of the place, the time, the occasion, of himself and natural ties, assailed the scared Narcisse, clutching him by the throat with the strength of a maniac, and pushing him backwards against the balustrade, and holding him there transfixed, while, with eyes seething with wrath beneath the blanched, and big, umbrageous brows, and showing like a sudden opening of the infernal pit, he cried: "Demon, degenerate dog, where hast thou been walking to and fro in the earth? whom helping to devour? Ah, son of Satan, ah! Aroint thee, Imp, Abortion."

The astonished wretch strove to reply, but terror and strangulation forbade him; and the enraged parent, like an incarnate storm, at arm's-length shook him, as the dog shakes the rat which it has caught, or the lion its prey; and each moment the shuddering youth, hearing his father's deep curses, and stiffening with horror, was urged further and yet further over the abyss, and still with aimless, outstretched arms, and disparted, claw-like fingers, strove to clutch the advocate's gown; while with upturned and beseeching eyes starting from their sockets, and still half on the balustrade and half in air, with nothing but the grasp of his adversary retaining him, he hung, while the arm that held him quivered, and surged uneasily from side to side, as if irresolute whether to plunge him or to draw him back; until a growl of satisfaction, followed by an execration, gurgling in the advocate's throat, announced the coming climax: the arm was jerked outwards, the clenched fingers unclutched themselves, like an automaton's, and the miserable mannikin tumbled with a yell down to the stones beneath. An instant all was silent, then a faint groan rose from the bruised form, that the next moment lay on the bloody flags a senseless corpse. Drawing a loud sigh of indescribable relief, after his fearful and protracted agitation, the advocate—and now murderer—stood glaring downwards with fixed eyes and yet clenched teeth; then, sickening at the horrid sight which loomed beneath, turned and leaned for support against the balustrade over which he had cast his child. Hearing the noise of the scuffle, some stragglers from the mixed crowd on the lobby came running to the spot, and one enquired of the

advocate if he were seized with a sudden sickness.
But he only pointed downwards to where lay his ill-
fated victim; and shook his head, looking all woe-
begone, in mad, mute misery. Astonished, some descended, and bearing the body up the stairs, laid it on
a bench that stood against the wall, and opposite its
destroyer; while a still increasing and motley multitude, including jurors, witnesses, constables, criers,
counsellors, clerks of the court, crown prosecutor, sheriff, and lastly, the judge himself, hurrying, gathered
round the scene of the catastrophe. A surgeon who
happened to have been subpœned upon the current
trial, opened a vein, but the blood refused to flow;
and a barrister, stripping himself of his gown, threw
it over the body as a pall. No one dared enquire the
origin of what he saw, until the judge arriving, demanded : " Who has done this ?"

" I," feebly answered the advocate, ghastly pale,
and yet leaning for support on the fatal balustrade.
Alas! what a change! His countenance was grown
haggard, and his white hair hung dishrevelled about
his collapsed visage, like icicles round the pinched
countenance of Winter. Despair was in his look,
and he uttered the name of Amanda, and gazed be-
wildered around him, as if awaking from a sorrowful
dream ; and now began to whimper, to gaze upon the
pall-like gown, and now to call upon the spirit that
had flown—as a scared bird from a bush—forth from
the body that lay beneath it.

" Narcisse," he feebly cried, " Narcisse, my son,
—for thou wert yet my son,—Narcisse, Narcisse," he
reiterated piteously ; and the Sheriff advanced in his
purple gown, and girt with his golden hilted sword,

laid his hand on the shoulder of the old man, the lately proud advocate, but now wretched culprit, as a sign of his being put under arrest. But none else moved; the Sheriff himself shrinking from ordering the constable to give effect to the signal. All seemed transfixed with pain or chained with horror, as in tremulous tones of touching tenderness the slayer continued to call upon the dead.

"Narcisse, my son, my son," he cried in agony; "Oh, I have killed thee, child; oh, thou art dead, dead, dead.—But thou didst steal thy sister; yes, I know thou didst; ay, that thou didst, and hast delivered her to dishonor, therefore have I killed thee. Come, Amanda, come hither, dearest, and behold thy brother; behold thy father, see what he has done, and all for thee. Yes, I did it, all you curious crowd. Amanda, oh, where art thou? let me see thee ere I die: Amanda dear, Amanda;" and at the words, Amanda, leaning on the arm of Claude, and followed by the elder Montigny and André Duchatel, appeared upon the corridor, a sweet smile playing upon her features, and hastening forwards she fell upon the neck of her guardian, who was still leaning against the balustrade, pale, haggard and forlorn. Her companions, restrained by astonishment and fear, gazed aloof and mute, whilst the wretched criminal, eyeing them with a look of misery and suspicion, in a tone of inexpressible sadness at length exclaimed:

"Come you to see me, then, before I die; do you come to triumph over me, Seigneur Montigny? Look, see there, but do not touch it, for it is abhorred, abominable, a foul spirit, a black imp of hell. Amanda, art thou found?—Do not tremble, girl, do not weep; my daughter, child, for, without a figure, thou art my daughter; art, to the very letter, love, my child. Oh, we have much to tell each other; see what I have done—but hear me, then condemn me. Oh, Amanda, it is bliss to see, to feel thee here;— but here, here in this breast is sadness. I have been a rash and hasty fool, a madman, if you will, but no, no murderer; we kill mere vermin, we exterminate rats, roaches; and what worse than that is this which I have done. Pshaw, he was a reptile, a black beetle that came flying against me. He, my son! Oh, slander, where wilt thou not cast thy slime? the thing that the deceitful, wily woman palmed upon me, he my son, thy brother? preposterous conception. Yet sad has been the creature's end; and sad, sad, sad, I felt this morning when I left my home, with a presentiment which seemed to say, that I should never enter it again; and that presentiment is now fulfilled. Fate urged me on. Unnatural hate has pushed me to the ledge, and now I sink to lose myself in the abyss. Oh, foul fate! this deed foul, foul! Fair, fair Amanda, close thine eyes on this enormity; or be content to see it, yet not understand it, for knowledge here would surely drive thee mad."

"Oh, sir, am I not mad, delirious?" enquired Amanda: "Oh, my kind guardian, my good angel, more than father, friend. What have you done? you have done nothing evil!" and she sobbed upon his bosom, and Claude stood transfixed and silent, until his eyes meeting those of the advocate, he demanded passionately:

"Sir, what may this mean; what horrible allusions drop like venom from your tongue; whence comes

this change; tell me, I charge you, sir, why are you
now so shaken, so wandering in your noble intellect,
even mad; you whom I left this morning, sad indeed,
yet sane ?"

"I do not know whether I was sane or not when
I did what I have done, or whether I am so just
now; but for this scene, which must appear most
strange to you, see there what shall explain it all,"
replied the advocate; and the gown was partially
withdrawn from the corpse by one of the spectators,
and Claude with his male companions gazed upon it
aghast, whilst Amanda turning away in terror and
uttering a feeble moan, hid her face in the old man's
breast.

"How has this happened ?"   Claude demanded at
last with a voice hoarse and guttural with abhorrence;
and the advocate shrugging his shoulders cynically
replied :

"A bruise, a fatal fall; strange that he should
have died of it.   It has been said, the lower in the
scale of being, the higher the tenacity of life.   Yet
here is an inferior intelligence dies of as little cor-
poreal damage, as might a poet or a philosopher.   There
is no certainty in speculation, for by this experiment
it has been proved, that the bulls-eye in the stable
window, in falling is as fragile as the palace's clearest
pane of crystal.   Who would have thought it?   A
dunce, that no one would have branded for having
brains, has from a mere tumble given up the ghost.
Bury him, bury him; I am sorry for it, but cannot
howl," and at these last words a howl was heard
from below, and soon Babet Blais came rushing along
the corridor, wringing her hands, and frantically

demanding : " Where is he, where is my boy, my
sweet Narcisse?" and threw herself upon the corpse
of her son. The advocate looked on with a bitter
smile, and when he beheld her covering with kisses
the cold, coarse features, exclaimed : " How these
things love each other !—but when he was alive she
would give him the food out of her mouth, draw for
him the blood from her veins, sacrifice the immortal
soul in her body with lies and patent perjury and
crookedest excuses, if so was that she might screen
him and his faults, deceiving me.—Beshrew thee,
woman !—but wherefore should I curse thee ? thou
art what thou wert made to be, even as I am that
which I was made to be, a desolation and a miserable
man :" and when he ceased Babet started from her
knees, and, looking on him with new born fierceness,
cried : " Monster, not master ; man killer, son killer,—
oh, you have killed my own, my dear Narcisse !
murdered my son, my boy, my child, my only joy :"
and she again cast herself upon the body, and, with
her face nestling in the dead bosom, sobbed and wept
aloud.

The advocate seemed softened, and, looking at
Claude, demanded : " Who is there that shall not
fulfil his fate ? for this I was born, and for it I shall
die." The sheriff again essayed to remove him, but he
sank at his touch, as the dust of an ancient corpse falls
before the breath of the outer atmosphere, and with
mortality moulding his visage: " Stay," he said, " let
me die here ; death has arrested me, he needs no
warrant." A spasm passed over his face, his frame
slightly quivered; and looking beseechingly at Claude,
the latter bent tenderly over him, and he thus began :

"It were foolish in me to suppose that you have not
heard of my irregularities. You will not be astonished, then, when I call this girl my child, no longer
my mere ward, but mine own child, so late acknowledged. Amanda, child,"—and his voice faltered,
while he spoke with increasing difficulty,—"will you
acknowledge me in this disgrace, receiving with the
name of father that of felon? Mona Macdonald is
your mother, to whom I have promised marriage till
my way down to perdition is paved with broken
oaths, as false as her love was true, and as hot as
was the fire which fell from heaven, when Elijah
strove with Baal's prophets, and that licked up the
water in the trench, as did those burning oaths of
mine so often dry up her tears. Give me your hand,
Claude; Seigneur Montigny, give me yours. I see a
change within you towards this lady. Stand not
between her and your son, as you would wish no sin
to stand betwixt yourself and Heaven at Judgment."
Then in a low tone meant only for Claude's ear,
he whispered, gasping :

"Think all I would have said, if there were time,
and we were happier. Farewell for ever; I cannot
tarry, neither would I do it now. I have outlived myself by near an hour, for I was not myself when I
performed this deed." And again a spasm passed
over his frame, his eyes grew fixed and glazed, and
he earnestly exclaimed : "Gather near me all who
love me, and all to love whom is my duty. Quick,
quick; for a film overspreads my eyes, the throes of
death are tearing down this frame. Quick, I am
dying. Bend over me; let me perceive your breath,
for I am blind. Bend, bend;—stoop yet lower; I

"Quick, I am dying; bend over me; let me perceive your breath, for I am blind."

cannot feel you, for each sense grows dull; stoop
lower yet.—Oh, soul, why all this haste? Amanda,
Claude, poor, missing Mona, I have somewhat more
to say to you; quick, listen, listen, or it will be too
late. Pshaw! pshaw! it *is* too late, too late, too
late!" And his head fell backwards, and with his
arms clasped convulsively around the necks of Claude
and Amanda, the advocate, like his son, was a corpse.

On the following day both of them were laid in
the English burying ground, but no stone marks the
spot, and in vain the stranger seeks to discover it.
None are able, or care, to point it out, restrained by
a superstitious awe. A few octogenarians still remember him, and look grave and shake the head,
when questioned as to the story and fate of the
talented and terrible Advocate of Montreal.

Lightning Source UK Ltd.
Milton Keynes UK
UKHW012359200722
406167UK00001B/282